RITUALS FOR A NEW AGE

Alternative Weddings, Funerals, Holidays, Etc.

Susan M. Mumm

Quantum Leap Publishing & Distributing, P.O. Box 7916, Ann Arbor, Michigan, 48107

Having come to view the universe is wholistic terms, I find it extremely difficult to write an acknowledgment page. In the truest sense, all the volumes of the ages could not contain the names of all the people/creatures who have made this small work possible.

My gratitude must begin with what I call God, the essence of all things. Yet, from there it becomes impossible to give thanks to everyone that it is due--a grandfather who questioned Christianity; a father who struggled to make meaning out of his existence and inspired me to do the same; a mother who gave me love; mentors who taught me to think analytically; a therapist who helped me work through old pains and get on with life; the wonderful friends who supported me and this endeavor through the years; my partner who suffered through my down times and believed in me, and cooked and cleaned for me while I worked seven days a week; my loving dogs who alleviated my terrible loneliness as I punched at a computer for nine hours a night--these are the obvious ones who helped this book to become a reality. However, what about the alcoholic bum who I passed on the street who made me question a system that could create and abandon such a person, the political activists who have died in struggles through the centuries and made my way of life possible, the farmers who grow my food, ad infinitum?

So--let me inadequately say--

A loving thank-you

to everyone who has made this possible.

susan m. mumm

Evolution

though sometimes subtle,

is eternal.

Contents

Chapter 4: Alternative Funeral Rituals..55

Chapter 5: Alternative Holiday Celebrations

Introduction

"Whatever possessed you to write a book about alternative rituals?" is a question I must have answered several hundred times over the course of the last five years. The process by which I became dissatisfied with the traditional rituals of our culture and interested in designing alternative rituals was a slow one, spanning fifteen years. My discontent heightened through the years as my political and religious beliefs diverged more and more from the typical values of United States culture. I began to discover again and again that the rituals I was participating in were based on values and beliefs in direct violation to my own. I found myself flinching each time I was confronted with the sexism, hierarchical power structures, and dogmatism of the churches, and the racism and classism of our government, which are inherent in the rituals of our culture.

My discomfort and dissatisfaction mounted until finally I realized I could no longer participate in the rituals of my culture because to do so violated the integrity of my being. I became determined to design some rituals for myself that were a reflection of my values. I wanted the ritual celebrations of my life to be times of spiritual rejuvenation; I wanted them to help me to clarify my life goals, regain balance and harmony with the universe, and to recapture my sense of joy in being alive. I was no longer willing for the rituals I was participating in to feel boring, alienating, and meaningless. I therefore started the challenging, confusing, and difficult but exciting process of designing alternative rituals for myself.

As I designed rituals for myself, I shared my ideas with friends. I was amazed at the overwhelming interest and enthusiasm I constantly met with regarding my alternative rituals. I discovered I was not alone in my disillusionment with traditional rituals. There were a lot of people out there who were disillusioned with traditional rituals and looking for alternatives. I was prompted by friends to perform on the radio, some of the rituals I had designed and I eventually did a live performance. All of these airings were enthusiastically received. It became obvious to everyone but me that I should write a book about alternative rituals. I can still fondly remember my close friend Everett Armstrong eagerly talking with me after we did a performance of my alternative marriage rituals. "Marriage rituals are just the beginning Susan--you should write a whole book of alternative rituals!"

After overcoming my initial lack of confidence about such an overwhelmingly difficult endeavor as writing a book, I realized it was in fact a good idea. I realized that by writing this book and explaining the process by which I became alienated with traditional rituals, I could hopefully help other people who were experiencing a vague, nebulous dissatisfaction about the rituals they are participating in, to clarify the reasons for their discontent. By sharing the discoveries and insights I reached about why traditional rituals no longer worked for me, I could help other people move from that initial stage of dreading Sunday church, funerals, weddings, and holidays, and not understanding why, to a clearer understanding of the reasons for their discontent. I could then present

1

some ideas about how to deal with this discontent!

In summary, this book is about my personal journey to redesign rituals more congruent with my needs and values. However, it is also an attempt to provide new rituals which embody the new spirituality and consciousness that is emerging--rituals free of sexism, racism, classism, and archaic, oppressive religious dogma. Only when our rituals and holiday celebrations reflect our values, can they serve the purpose they are meant to: to re-inspire us to structure our lives and relationships so as to maximize our fullest potential as human beings. I hope this book will help you to reclaim the rituals in your lives as times of joyful celebration.

Chapter 1

Why Alternative Rituals?

The process by which I became dissatisfied with the traditional rituals of our culture and interested in designing alternative rituals happened over a period of many years. My ever-increasing discontent with the rituals of our culture was a result of the dramatic and fundamental changes I underwent over the years regarding my political and religious beliefs. The rituals of a culture are a major way in which the political/religious values of that society are subtly but powerfully reinforced. Inherent in rituals are a myriad of religious precepts: definitions of God, God's relation to humanity, assumptions about life and how to live it, views about relationships between men and women, afterlife, and so on. Also inherent in rituals are political values: assumptions about relationships among societal members, distribution of resources, and decision-making power, to cite a few. As my religious and political beliefs diverged more and more from the norm in the United States, I found myself more and more dissatisfied with traditional rituals because they reinforced values that were in direct violation to my own. Therefore, in order to explain why I felt impelled to stop participating in the traditional rituals of our culture, I need to discuss how and why I came to disagree with the religious and political precepts on which the rituals of our culture are based. I will outline briefly, then, the changes I have undergone regarding my religious and political beliefs, which eventually led to my discontent with traditional rituals and subsequent writing of this book.

Having grown up in a culture heavily influenced by Christianity, I viewed the universe through Christian eyes for many years. I believed in God the Father, I believed <u>The Bible</u> to be the word of God, that Jesus was God's Son sent to teach us about God's expectations, in Heaven and Hell, and on and on. However, sometime in my early twenties, I was beginning to have some doubts about a lot of these concepts. I wasn't sure exactly what about them didn't feel right, but I was beginning to feel more and more uncomfortable. I read, re-read, and re-read <u>The Bible</u> and listened to sermon after sermon, trying to sort out my confusing thoughts and feelings about the teachings of Christianity. I was very impressed and moved by some of what I read in <u>The Bible.</u> Whenever I read Jesus's teachings about forgiveness, unconditional love, or living a life of voluntary simplicity, I would feel a deep conviction that these were truths of the universe which I, if I was going to find any peace and harmony, needed to live by. Yet there were many other teachings that, try as I might, I could not believe to be true. I found it very difficult to sort out what made sense to me and what didn't.

The reason it took me so long to verbalize and clarify my disagreements with Christianity was because I was afraid that I would incur the wrath of Almighty God and burn in hellfire forever. How dare I even consider the idea that some of the ideas of <u>The Bible</u> could be right and others not? Did I not understand that every word was divinely inspired straight from the all-knowing God the Father? One did not question and negotiate truth with God, not the Christian God. The obvious reason I was disagreeing with some of <u>The Bible's</u> teachings, was that I was a weak sinner with no will power, clearly under the influence of Satan. Hopefully I would come to my senses before God returned to this planet to gather up His obedient followers who had the good sense to follow His divine directives about how to live. I had better stop sinning; otherwise I would be gathered along with the rest of the sinning questioners and sent to my deserved Hell. So for years I battled with my

3

confusion. Was The Bible the divine word of God, or was it not? Somehow, after a lot of agonizing, I decided it was not. I would sometimes literally shake with fear that I was making the biggest mistake of my life as I began parting ways with Christianity.

It's difficult to re-trace the exact steps I took away from Christianity, since the process began over fifteen years ago. I recall turning points, like in 1972, when at the height of the feminist movement Helen Reddy won the Grammy Award for her song "I Am Woman" and wryly joked in her thank-you speech, "...and lastly, I would like to thank God. She's been a great help all along the way." Getting in touch with how absurd the idea was that God was a paternal fatherly being was thus a beginning. As I read more about feminism and radical politics, I began to understand how and why God had come to be depicted as a powerful, omnipotent male figure. The God portrayed in Christianity began to appear more and more to me like an archaic myth, invented to uphold an oppressive patriarchal system.

As a feminist, I could no longer live with the idea of God being portrayed as a male. Therefore I did some exploring into what is known as "Feminist Spirituality." I began exploring Goddess-centered religions. I began reading books like The Spiral Dance: A Rebirth of the Ancient Religion of The Great Goddess by Starhawk, The First Sex by Elizabeth Gould Davis, and The Woman's Encyclopedia of Myths and Secrets by Barbara G. Walker. It was a totally mind-boggling experience to learn that before the advent of patriarchy there had been matriarchal societies. How startling to read that before Christianity, with its central theme of a male/father ruler/creator of the universe, there had been religions which depicted the universe as being created and maintained by a female Goddess. Moreover, these Goddess-centered religions were common throughout the world for many, many centuries. Many of my more radical feminist friends were exploring Witchcraft, there having been a great resurgence in this Goddess-centered religion. Some of my friends became witches with their own covens, rituals, etc..

However, after doing a great deal of reading in feminist spirituality, I found I had some major disagreements with many of the basic concepts. As I read the creation myths and religious concepts of Goddess-centered religions, I observed a lot of reverse sexism. I had become very sensitized to the subtleties of sexism from learning to recognize anti-female sexism, and thus I was very aware of the anti-male bias that I continually found in the Goddess-centered religions. Exploring these ancient religions made me aware of whole segments of history (herstory) where women had dominated religion and politics. I was shocked, however, to discover again and again that women had treated men with the same disregard, disrespect, and inequality of which men in this age are guilty. It appeared to me that throughout history there had been a spiral of dominance/oppression, with the role of oppressor and oppressed flipping back and forth between men and women. I felt deep in my soul that the time at last was here when the potential existed for men and women to break out of this destructive cycle of sexism and power struggle and come to peace. Sonja Johnson expressed this sentiment well in her book From Housewife To Heretic:

But personally I am not willing to replace the patriarchal Old Testament God with the matriarchal one that preceded him....What is the use of exchanging one brand of sexism for another? Many women who are sensitive to the phenomenon of god-discovery going on are also concerned lest we women, in our turn, exclude men from deity as men have so devastatingly excluded us.

Now that we are undertaking the long overdue reorganization of heaven, we must make sure there is a model there, and a representative there, for every human being. Everyone must be empowered, because we

4

have sons and husbands and brothers and fathers as well as sisters, mothers, and daughters. Surely we must hate disenfranchisement so much that we will never inflict it upon anyone else. None of us is free so long as anyone is oppressed.

Sonja Johnson, <u>From Housewife To Heretic</u>, New York, Double Day, 1983, pp. 378-79.

I thus had to reject both Christianity because of its sexism against women, and Goddess-centered religions because of their sexism against men. I was interested in a religion/spirituality that was free of sexism. In order to view God in non-sexist terms I evolved away from the idea of God being a personality at all. Rather I was beginning to see God as more of an energy. I was finding it difficult to define for myself what exactly God was, yet I sensed there was something out there that created and kept the universe in harmony. Finally, I happened upon a definition of God that put into words what I was struggling to conceptualize, in a book entitled <u>Seth Speaks; The Eternal Validity Of The Soul</u> by Jane Roberts: [1]

...When you consider the question of a supreme being, you imagine a male personality with those abilities that you yourself possess, with great emphasis upon qualities you admire. This imagined god has therefore changed throughout your centuries mirroring man's shifting ideas of himself.

God was seen as cruel and powerful when man believed that these were desirable characteristics, needed particularly in his battle for physical survival. He projected these upon his idea of a god because he envied them and feared them. You have cast your idea of god, therefore, in your own image.

In a reality that is inconceivably multidimensional, the old concepts of god are <u>relatively</u> meaningless. Even the term, a supreme being, is in itself distortive, for you naturally project the qualities of human nature upon it. If I told you that God was an idea, you would not understand what I meant, for you do not understand the dimensions in which an idea has its reality, or the energy that it can originate and propel. You do not believe in ideas in the same way that you believe in physical objects, so if I tell you that God is an idea, you will misinterpret this to mean that God is less than real--nebulous, without reality, without purpose, and without motive action.

Now your own physical image is the materialization of your <u>idea</u> of yourself within the properties of matter. Without the idea of yourself, your physical image would not be; yet often it is all you are aware of. The initial power and energy of that idea of yourself keeps your image alive. Ideas, then, are far more important than you realize. If you will try to accept the idea that your own existence is multidimensional, that you dwell within the medium of infinite probabilities, then you may catch a slight glimpse of the reality that is behind the word "god", and you may understand why it is almost impossible to capture a true understanding of that concept in words.

God, therefore, is first of all a creator, not of one physical universe, but of an infinite variety of probable existences, far more vast than those aspects of the physical universe with which your scientists are familiar. He did not simply then send a son to live and die on one small planet. He is a part of all probabilities.

...God is more than the sum of all the probable systems of reality

He has created, and yet He is within each one of these, without exception. He is therefore within each man and woman. He is also within each spider, shadow, and frog, and that is what man does not like to admit.

God can only be experienced, and you experience Him whether or not you realize it, through your own existence. He is not male or female, however, and I use the term only for convenience's sake. In the most inescapable truth, he is not human in your terms at all, nor in your terms is He a personality. Your ideas of personality are too limited to contain the multitudinous facets of His multidimensional existence.

On the other hand, He is human, in that He is a portion of each individual; and within the vastness of His experience He holds an "idea-shape" of Himself as human, to which you can relate. He literally was made flesh to dwell among you, for He forms your flesh in that He is responsible for the energy that gives vitality and validity to your private multidimensional self....

...All That Is [this is Seth's word for God] is not done and finished. All That Is simultaneously and unendingly creates Itself. ...There is no "perfect ending," no completed perfection beyond which further experience is impossible or meaningless. All That Is is a source of infinite and unending simultaneous action. Everything happens at once, and yet there is no beginning and end to it in your terms, so it is not completed in your terms at any given point.

Your idea of development and growth, again, implies a one-line march towards perfection, so it would be difficult for you to imagine the kind of order that pervades. Ultimately a completed or finished God, or All That Is, would end up smothering His creation. For perfection presupposes that point beyond which development is impossible, and creativity at an end.

There would be an order in which only predestination could rule, each part fitting in with a particular order without freedom to change the pattern given it. There is order, but within this order there is freedom--the freedom of creativity, that characteristic of All That Is, that guarantees Its infinite becoming.

Now in that infinite becoming, there are states that you would call perfected, but had creativity rested within them, all of experience would be destined to grind to a halt. Yet this great complexity is not unwieldy; it is as simple, in fact, as a seed."

Jane Roberts, Seth Speaks; The Eternal Validity Of The Soul, pp. 240, 241, 242, 245, 356. Reprinted by permission of the publisher, Prentice-Hall, Inc., Englewoods Cliffs, NJ 07632.

AUTHOR'S NOTE:
Please disregard the sexist language e.g., "man" for humanity, "he" for she/he. Seth repeatedly makes references to the fact that he uses these sexist terms to speed dictation. He states several times that God is neither male nor female.

Reading these Seth books was an important catalyst in helping me to redefine God in a way that made sense to me. Seth's ideas of God being a creative energy, or idea, was much more of a workable concept to me than was the Father personality type God of Christianity. Being prompted by Seth to reconceptulize God as an energy, as opposed to a personified deity, also impelled me to reconsider all of the characteristics of God I had learned from Christianity.

The first Characteristic of God that I began reconsidering, after letting go of the concept of God as a male father figure, was the idea of a wrathful God who demanded blind obedience. That concept permeates The Bible from Adam and Eve throughout the chapters. The very idea of a God who sends a messenger to tell us how to live is a God who expects obedience. Over and over again I wondered why God would have given me this intuitive, questioning mind, a mind that longs to come to my own conclusions as a result of my own experiences, and then expect and want me not to use it. How could God expect human beings not to follow that unquenchable desire to learn for themselves, to continue to interpret reality? Why would God damn me to Hell for thinking for myself? How could the purpose of this existence be to overcome all my desires to think and question and to become an obedient follower of every word of The Bible, in order to someday go to Heaven? And what would I do in Heaven anyway--play harps all day, having finally acquired "bliss", like George Winston in George Orwell's famous novel 1984, after he had given up thinking and fighting? Somehow I didn't buy it. Slowly I began putting together from various readings that this wrathful obedience-demanding God was just an invention of people who used the concept to wield power for themselves. The concepts of Christianity that had always puzzled and discontented me slowly began to make perfect sense when viewed in a historical political perspective. I can best communicate the sense of freedom and relief I experienced as I let go of the oppressive God of Christianity, by including the following poem by James Kavanaugh in which he expresses so beautifully the sense of freedom he experienced upon his similar experience of letting go of the wrathful God of Christianity:

My Easy God Is Gone

I have lost my easy God--the one whose name
    I knew since childhood.
I knew his temper, his sullen outrage, his
    ritual forgiveness.
I knew the strength of his arm, the sound
    of his insistent voice.
His beard bristling, his lips full and red
    with moisture at the moustache,
His eyes clear and piercing, too blue
    to understand all,
His face too unwrinkled to feel my
    child's pain.
He was a good God--so he told me--
    a long suffering and manageable one.
I knelt at his feet and kissed them,
    I felt the smooth countenance of his forgiveness.

I never told him how he frightened me,
    How he followed me as a child
When I played with friends or begged
    for candy on Halloween.
He was a predictable God, I was the
    unpredictable one.

He was unchanging, omnipotent, all-seeing,
        I was volatile and helpless.

He taught me to thank him for the concern
        which gave me no chance to breathe,
For the love which demanded only love in
        return--and obedience.
He made pain sensible and patience possible
        and the future foreseeable.
He, the mysterious, took all mystery away,
        corroded my imagination,
Controlled the stars and would not let
        them speak for themselves.

Now he haunts me seldom: some fierce
        umbilical is broken,
I live with my own fragile hopes and
        sudden rising despair.
Now I do not weep for my sins; I have
        learned to love them
And to know that they are the wounds that
        make love real.
His face illudes me; his voice, with all
        its pity, does not ring in my ear.
His maxims memorized in boyhood do not
        make fruitless and pointless my experience.
I walk alone, but not so terrified as when
        he held my hand.

I do not splash in the blood of his son
        nor hear the crunch of nails or thorns
        piercing protesting flesh.
I am a boy again--I whose boyhood was
        turned to manhood in a brutal myth.
Now wine is only wine with drops that do
        not taste of blood.
The bread I eat has too much pride for
        transubstantiation,
I, too--and together the bread and I embrace,
        Each grateful to be what we are, each loving
        from our own reality.
Now the bread is warm in my mouth and
        I am warm in its mouth as well.

Now my easy God is gone--he knew too
        much to be real,
He talked too much to listen, he knew
        my words before I spoke.
But I knew his answers as well--computerized
        and turned to dogma
His stamp was on my soul, his law locked
        cross-like on my heart,
His imperatives tattooed on my breast, his
        aloofness canonized in ritual.

Now he is gone--my easy, stuffy God--God,
        the father-master, the mother-whiner, the
Dull, whoring God who offered love bought
        by an infant's fear.
Now the world is mine with all its pain and
        warmth, with its every color and sound;
The setting sun is my priest with the ocean
        for its altar.
The rising sun redeems me with the rolling
        waves warmed in its arms.
A dog barks and I weep to be alive, a
        cat studies me and my joy is boundless.
I lie on the grass and boy-like, search the sky.
        The clouds do not turn to angels, the winds
        do not whisper of heaven or hell.

Perhaps I have no God--what does it matter?
        I have beauty and joy and
        transcending loneliness,
I have the beginning of love--as beautiful as it
        is feeble--as free as it is human.
I have the mountains that whisper secrets
        held before men could speak,
I have the ocean that belches life on
        the beach and caresses it in the sand,
I have a friend who smiles when he sees
        me, who weeps when he hears my pain,
I have a future full of surprises, a
        present full of wonder.
I have no past--the steps have disappeared
        the wind has blown them away.

I stand in the Heavens and on earth, I
        feel the breeze in my hair.
I can drink to the North Star and shout
        on a bar stool,
I can feel the teeth of a hangover, the
        joy of laziness,
The flush of my own rudeness, the surge of
        my own ineptitude.
And I can know my own gentleness as well,
        my wonder, my nobility.
I sense the call of creation, I feel its
        swelling in my hands.
I can lust and love, eat and drink, sleep
        and rise,
But my easy God is gone--and in his stead
        The mystery of loneliness and love!

9

Like James Kavanaugh so aptly expresses above, I found that as I became free of my obedience-demanding Christian God, my view of the entire universe, and my role within it became transformed. I was ready to replace my old "easy God" with a new God. This new God I was learning about wasn't interested in dictating my feelings, thoughts and life. This new God of mine hadn't dictated all of life's answers into a "Holy Book" and wasn't going to be awaiting me at death to judge whether or not I had followed the directives to His satisfaction. Rather, this new God of mine had blessed me with the freedom to experience life in my unique way and find my own answers and path. What an awesome responsibility to suddenly be confronted with. This new God was wonderful and exciting yet also mind-boggling:

I do not tell you that a God is waiting for you on the other side of a golden door. I do not reassure you by telling you that when you are dead, God will be waiting for you in all His majestic mercy, and that that will be the end of your responsibility. And so as I said last evening, in my latest chapter, I offer no hope for the lazy, for they will not find eternal rest.

However, through traveling within yourselves, you will discover the unity of your consciousness with other consciousnesses. You will discover the multidimensional love and energy that gives consciousness to all things. This will not lead you to want to rest upon the proverbial blessed bosom. It will instead inspire you to take a better hand in the job of creation; and that feeling of divine presence you will find indeed, and feel indeed, for you will sense it behind the dance of the molecules, and in yourselves and in your neighbors. What so many want is a God who walks down the street and says, "Happy Sunday, I am I, follow me." But God is hidden craftily in His creations, so that He is what they are and they are what He is; and in knowing them, you know him.

...You are the power of God manifested. You are not powerless. To the contrary. Through your being the power of God is strengthened, for you are a portion of what He is. You are not simply an insignificant, innocuous clump of clay through which He decided to show Himself. You are He manifesting as you. You are as legitimate as He is. If you are a part of God then He is also a part of you, and in denying your own worth you end up denying His as well. I do not like to use the term "He", meaning God, since All That Is [This is Seth's word for God.] is the origin of not only all sexes but of all realities, in some of which sex as you think of it does not exist.

...You do not have to die to find God. All That Is, is now, and you are a part of All That Is now. As I have told you often, you are a spirit <u>now.</u> The avenues for development are open <u>now.</u>

...You are a multidimensional personality. Trust the miracle of your own being. Make no divisions between the physical and the spiritual in your lifetimes, for the spiritual speaks with a physical voice and the corporeal body is the creation of the spirit.

Do not place the words of gurus, ministers, priests, scientists, psychologists, friends--or my words--higher than the feelings of your own being. You can learn much from others, but the deepest knowledge must come from within yourself.

...Trust no person who tells you that you are evil or guilty by reason of your nature or your physical existence, or any such dogma. Trust no one who leads you away from the reality of yourself. Do not follow those who tell you that you must do penance, in whatever form.

Trust instead the spontaneity of your own being and the life that is your own.

...Your own consciousness is embarked upon a reality that basically can be experienced by no other, that is unique and untranslatable, with its own meaning, following its own paths of becoming.

You share an existence with others who are experiencing their own journeys, in their own ways, and you have journeying in common, then. Be kind to yourself and to your companions.

...I close by saying, as I have said before: You are given the gift of the gods; you create your reality according to your beliefs; yours is the creative energy that makes your world; there are no limitations to the self except those you believe in.

...You create your life through the inner power of your being, whose source is within you and yet beyond the selves that you know. Use those creative abilities with understanding abandon. Honor yourselves and move through the godliness of your being."

Jane Roberts, <u>Seth Speaks; The Eternal Validity Of The Soul</u>, pp. 480, 482.

Jane Roberts, <u>The Nature Of Personality</u>, pp. 482, 506, 508, 509. Reprinted by permission of the publisher, Prentice-Hall, Inc., Englewood Cliffs, NJ 07632.

Now, at long last, I am going to explain how all these esoteric ramblings about God relate to the subject of this book--rituals. Having acquired a belief system which was in many ways diametrically opposed to most of the basic tenets of Christianity, I became more and more dissatisfied with many of the rituals of our society because of their inherent Christian nature. The rituals represented concepts of God, God's relationship to humanity, male/female relationships and a view of life, (both on this plane and beyond), that were in total contradiction to my ideas.

The first ritual I became dissatisfied with, quite understandably, was going to Sunday services at Christian churches. I was no longer interested in rehashing and reinterpreting <u>The Bible</u>, as I no longer believed it to be the word of God. I felt I had gotten everything I could get from <u>The Bible</u>. I still thought it contained many valuable spiritual teachings. Though I no longer saw Jesus as a messenger from God in the traditional sense, I still saw him as a great spiritual teacher. However, I was ready to explore an infinite number of other teachings as well. I came to believe that I could be spiritually enlightened by the teachings of many, many people and by my own internal meditations. I was thus becoming very unhappy with the idea of going to church every Sunday to have Jesus's teachings endlessly regurgitated to me.

Not only was I bored with the content of the Sunday sermons but I could also no longer tolerate the fundamental structure of the churches themselves. Their inherent hierarchical elitist power structure violated my values. I could no longer endure the idea of the minister being set up on a pedestal as the expert, as having some special "in" with God. I was no longer interested in coming week after week to hear the minister impart his/her "wisdom" to the congregation. I no longer believed that simply by virtue of their position, that clergy know more about spiritual matters than the rest of us. What I was interested in was an egalitarian coming together with other people to explore an unending variety of spiritual teachings, as well as our own personal revelations.

For a while, I experimented with attending the Universalist Unitarian church. This church was much more compatible with my evolving spiritual beliefs. There is little dogma; the spiritual beliefs of Unitarians are varied, ranging from atheism to semi-Christian to individualized religious theories. Furthermore, there is no pressure put on anyone to conform to a particular set of beliefs. Unitarian Universalist churches are each set up as a member-owned and operated democracy--one person, one vote. They elect their board of directors and hire and fire their own ministers. The church holds many interesting discussion groups about a variety of subjects in addition to the regular Sunday services. Instead of celebrating traditional Christian holidays, e.g. Christmas and Easter, they celebrate the solstices and equinoxes. However, I soon became discontent with the Unitarian Universalist church too. Though the ministers were definitely more liberal (by a long shot), and "free-thinking", there was still a hierarchy implicit in the structure of even the U.U. church that I became more and more uncomfortable with. The ministers were still set apart as being experts. They stood up every Sunday to impart their spiritual wisdom to the congregation. This, like the idea of Jesus having an exclusive monopoly on God's wisdom, violated my beliefs.

Next I briefly explored Judaism. I was attracted to Judaism because I too, did not believe Jesus to be "the Christ." However, as I further clarified my beliefs, I realized I had major differences with Judaism too. I had come to disagree with the concept of a Christ at all. Though Jews do not belive Jesus to be the Christ, they believe that there will someday be a messiah who will come to us. I disagreed with the concept of a messiah. In general, I found Judaism to be very similar to Christianity, and this is understandable since one grew out of the other. As was the case with Christianity, I was turned off by the sexism, hierarchical structure, and rigidity of Judaism.

I next explored the Quaker Society of Friends. Several of my friends were familiar with the structure of the Quaker Society of Friends and suggested I explore the Friends Society in Ann Arbor where I lived. I was extremely impressed with the structure of their worship services. Their meetings are held in circles, and all members participate. There is no minister, and facilitation of the meeting is rotated. However, I found that the Quaker Society of Friends was still too tied to Christianity for me. Their structure is very different from typical Christian churches, but far too many of their ideas still revolve around the concept of Jesus being the one and only Christ. I found therefore, that I was not satisfied attending Friends' meetings either. I was discovering over and over again that the more liberal/radical religions were trying to re-package and upgrade Christianity, yet they were still inside a box; I wanted out of the confining box of Christianity.

After exploring a great number of churches and concluding that I couldn't be satisfied with any of them because my religious beliefs were too incompatible, I was challenged to develop a replacement for the ritual of Sunday church service in my life. I therefore set up with a group of friends what might be called a "spiritual attunement" group. Instead of going to church each Sunday to "connect" with God via the clergy, we as a group met weekly to learn how to connect with the God within each of us. Instead of looking to the clergy for spiritual answers, we began to help one another discover our own spiritual answers. Our attunement group covered topics which ranged from afterlife, to good and evil, to sexuality, to reincarnation, to ....

Participating in this group greatly enhanced my growth on a spiritual, emotional and intellectual level. Through the years I have continued to participate in a spiritual attunement group on a regular basis. It has been so much more rewarding to me than those stale Christian church services I sat through for so many years. If you have stopped going to church because your beliefs have become incompatible, but miss coming together with a group for the sense of community, I recommend that you form an attunement group. In the chapter "In Lieu of Sunday Church Service: Attunement, Affinity, Personal Growth, and Consciousness Raising Groups", I have put together information to help you get a group started. There is a list of recommended topics you might want to use to get the group started as well as a selection of readings that could be used for group discussion. I think you will be amazed at how eagerly your friends and acquaintances will respond to an invitation to join a group.

Deciding not to participate in the ritual of going to church every Sunday was just a first step, however. I soon discovered that I was becoming increasingly discontent with other rituals of our culture as well, i.e. rites of passage. For example, wedding ceremonies in the United States are imbued with Judeo-Christian values. All Christian marriage rituals are set up as a life-long covenant between the couple and God. "Those God has joined together, let no man put asunder." However, the God I have come to believe in has granted me the freedom to decide on the particulars of my life. Thus, I don't believe any longer that God has sent down a directive that life-long marriage is the only correct way to live.

From my own life experiences, I had come to believe that I could not predict that a life-long marriage would necessarily be the option most conducive to my happiness. I had come to realize that as men and women grow and change and move along the evolutionary paths they are each called to follow throughout the course of their lives, they may find that they change in ways that prevent them from meeting each other's needs as lovers. Though I believed that some people might best manifest their potential as human beings within the context of a fifty-year marriage, I firmly believed that for other people to have several partnerships throughout the course of their lives would be the option most conducive to their growth and happiness. I thus did not think it made any sense for me to pledge in a marriage ritual "I take you as my husband till death do us part" because I had no way of knowing how we would each grow and change in the years ahead.

Another aspect of Christian marriage rituals that I was extremely dissatisfied with was their inherent sexism. I found the idea of obeying my husband and viewing him "as the head of the marriage, as Christ is the head of the church", an appalling concept. In addition, I disagreed with the whole idea of the church having the power/authority to marry me. Being thus dissatisfied with traditional marriage rituals, I designed an alternative ritual several years ago. This alternative "marriage" ritual and a discussion of the reasoning behind it is included in the chapter "Alternative Marriage Rituals."

After weddings, I next tackled funerals, as they were another ritual I had for many years been extremely dissatisfied with. Having parted ways with Christianity, the thought had occurred to me more than once that I would not at all like my surviving family to give a typical Christian funeral on my behalf when I died. I wasn't exactly sure what kind of funeral ceremony I wanted held in my behalf, but I knew I didn't want some Christian minister being called in to rant and rave about how I had gone to Heaven to play harps with God the Father. I was thus interested in designing a funeral ritual, as I thought it would be comforting to know that when I died the service given for me would reflect my spiritual orientation.

I felt very much at a loss, however, when I initially sat down to try to write the funeral chapter. I wasn't at all sure what I thought a funeral ritual should be like, having never been to a non-Christian funeral. I found I had to do a lot of soul searching in order to design an alternative funeral service. It forced me to clarify, even further, my thoughts about God, afterlife, etc. I also ended up doing a lot of research about the laws regarding funerals. In the funeral chapter I have included legal information about planning an alternative funeral, a guideline for facilitating an alternative funeral service, two sample funeral services, as well as a collection of spiritual readings appropriate for funerals.

I have discussed thus far my religious disagreements with the rituals of our culture. Part of my dissatisfaction with rituals also stemmed from changes in my political beliefs, since rituals have a political as well as religious significance. My political beliefs had undergone many dramatic changes through the years. How does one explain living through the sixties and early seventies? My views of many, many things were transformed in very profound ways. Feminism, the anti-war/world peace movement, the ecology movement, Watergate, world hunger awareness, nuclear threat, black power, rock and roll, drugs, the sexual revolution, and voluntary simplicity; these revolutionary ideas radically altered my political views. Unlike some people for whom "being a hippie" as you might call it, was a stage they went through and left behind, for me the changes were permanent. My politics continued to be radical. As my political views changed, I became more and more unhappy with many of the holiday rituals of our culture. Let me cite as an example Columbus Day. I, like all United States school-children, was taught to admire Columbus. I have vague grade school memories of little poems like, "In fourteen hundred and ninety two, Columbus sailed the ocean blue", and I still know the names of his ships. However, through the years as I read history books like Howard Zinn's A People's History of the United States, the picture painted of Columbus was far from my idea of heroic. As I read about the atrocities perpetrated by Columbus upon Native Americans, I realized that by continuing to acknowledge/celebrate Columbus Day, I was subtly reinforcing racism and colonialism. When a black friend of mine sarcastically joked "How in the hell can you discover a country that's already inhabited?", I became even more aware of the inherent racism surrounding Columbus's heroization. Another example of a holiday I came to disagree with for political reasons is "The Fourth of July". To my mind, it is a tragic irony to celebrate that we in the United States are free of colonial rule and taxation, when we have become one of the most powerful and oppressive colonizers in the world today. As I became aware of the gruesome practices the U.S. government perpetrates upon the people of Third World countries in order to rape them of resources, I found I could not take any joy in celebrating our freedom from colonization by England. Also, when I reflected upon how long it took for the beautiful and flowery language of the Declaration of Independence to have any real effect and meaning for blacks, women, and other oppressed minorities, celebrating the Fourth of July appeared to me to be a sham. I began to understand that holiday rituals are one of the ways in which cultural norms are subtly reinforced and I wanted to make sure I wasn't unconsciously helping to uphold cultural norms like racism and sexism.

I made a decision to reexamine each of the holiday rituals I was participating in and to reconsider whether the rituals were congruent with my political/religious beliefs. I realized it was particularly important that I examine the holiday rituals I was participating in before I began raising children, so that I didn't pass on to my children holiday rituals that subtly reinforced values in direct violation of my own. I therefore took out a calendar one day and wrote down all the major holidays, both secular and non-secular, listed on a typical United States calendar. I then spent several months researching the origins of the holidays and thinking about whether or not what they represented was meaningful to me. I made a decision to no longer celebrate any holiday which violated my religious/political beliefs. I eliminated some holiday celebrations from my life, and redesigned others to better meet my needs. I also made up a few new ones. In the chapter "Alternative Holiday Celebrations", I discuss each major holiday celebration of our culture. I discuss why I have decided to celebrate or not celebrate it, and I also include my ideas for alternative holidays where appropriate.

In summary, I designed these alternative rituals because I needed new rituals to reflect the new views I had come to regarding many, many things: God, male/female relationships, afterlife, power relationships and resource allocation within society etc., etc. Designing the rituals to be congruent with my political/religious beliefs, however, was not easy. I didn't want my rituals to be rigid or dogmatic. Thus, in designing these rituals, I have tried to draw from a huge variety of sources: Seth's ideas, Buddhist concepts, Witchcraft, Christianity, Communism, Quakerism, Psychology

14

101 classes, and who knows what else. Lastly, I have tried to design rituals that are open and flowing so that they are easily changed and adapted. What makes sense today in terms of rituals may appear archaic and outdated in ten years, or for that matter, one year from now. Through the process of thinking, feeling, and living each day of my life, I hope I will come to a continually new understanding of God, myself, life, the universe, ad infinitum. I will therefore always need my rituals to reflect my new and ever-changing beliefs.

Footnotes: Chapter 1

1) Jane Roberts was (she died in 1984), a psychic medium from Elmira, New York, who with her husband Robert Butts wrote a substantial number of books. Jane is a channel for an entity from another dimension named Seth. If the idea of communicating with entities from other dimensions sounds unbelievable to you I encourage you to read Seth Speaks: The Eternal Validity of The Soul or The Nature of Personal Reality both by Jane Roberts. I find the ideas presented in these books about God, death, afterlife, reincarnation, right and wrong etc. to make more sense than than any other religious theory I have ever come across. They are available at most book stores.

Chapter 2

In Lieu Of Sunday Church Service:

Attunement / Affinity / Rap / Co-Counseling / Personal Growth / Consciousness-Raising Groups.

It has been many, many years since I made a decision not to go to "Sunday Services" at Christian churches. I would like to share my dissatisfactions about going to church and share some information about the exciting alternatives to church I have discovered. I hope that in doing so I can help other people who have left the churches in search of something more in tune with their values to become aware of the many wonderful alternatives to church that have come into being.

My decision to stop participating in church was a result of my reaching a point at which my values/beliefs were so diametrically opposed to the teachings of Christianity, that I could no longer feel comfortable within the church structure. Since I described in detail in Chapter 1 my growing away from Christianity, I will just briefly summarize it here.

Year after year, I continued to find that I had more and more disagreements with Christianity. The ways I perceived God and the relationship I believed existed between God and humanity was fundamentally different from the concepts Christianity taught. I also no longer perceived Jesus to have been a christ, that is, a special messenger from God. I simply viewed Jesus as one of many human beings who had some very valuable and enlightened ideas. In addition, my views about after-life, ethics, the purpose of life, and male/female relationships among others, were in direct opposition to Christianity.

Perhaps most importantly, I had come to disagree with the whole concept of a clergy. I no longer believed that clergy people had some special channel to God. I believed that all human beings were capable of communicating with God. I thus found the hierarchical structure of the churches unnecessary, oppressive, and stifling. Finding myself so completely at odds with Christianity, I made a decision, in my early twenties, to find a replacement for Christian Church services in my life.

Initially, I even wondered whether the whole concept of coming together as a group made sense. Would I rather just go out in the woods every Sunday morning by myself and tune into God, or perhaps read a spiritual book every week? I eventually came to the conclusion that both spending time by myself meditating and reading and coming together with a group of people to discuss spiritual/religious issues were important to have as part of my life. I could learn a lot from turning inward, but I could also benefit greatly from exchanging ideas with other people. Therefore, I was interested in setting up a spiritual study group in which we, as a group, could explore an infinite variety of spiritual teachings and get in touch with the divinity in ourselves.

For several years my religious group study was rather informal. I would just get together with friends and bring up "heavy" spiritual and philosophical topics. However, I came to desire something a little more structured. I decided to try to put together a group which would meet on a regular basis. Therefore, in my senior year of college, I organized weekly pot-luck dinner/discussion groups. I jokingly told all my friends that if they had grown tired and bored of blas'e, and superficial dinner party conversation, I had just the thing for them. I began sending out invitations every week which read something like this:

You are invited to a dinner/discussion group. Bring a dish to share.
Topic for the evening will be:

Do you believe in an after-life? Why or why not? If yes, describe what
you think existence is like after death.   Also describe how you think
this life affects what happens to you after you die.

I was surprised and pleased at the response I got. I introduced a variety of
topics and had approximately ten people every week. It was amazing how eagerly
people responded to the opportunity to share their innermost feelings and
philosophical introspections. Some examples of other questions I used in those
discussion groups were:

Do you believe in a God? Share your definition of God.

Do you believe God intervenes in human affairs? Do you feel you have
ever communicated with God? Describe.

Do you believe God sends messengers/spiritual teachers, i.e., Jesus?

You were informed this week that you are terminally ill and have only a
month to live. You have been asked to speak for a half-hour on what
you consider the most important spiritual insights you have reached in
your life.

Do you believe in reincarnation? Do you have any memory of former
lives?

Have you ever had an "out of body" experience?

Sue Mumm's "kookie" dinner parties got to be quite the rage. It was wonderful
to have the opportunity to talk with people about such subjects.
Groups such as these are becoming increasingly popular. More and more
people are reaching the same conclusions that I did; that they are no longer
interested in having religious dogma preached to them.   Rather they are
interested in discovering and formulating their own answers based on their
life experiences.   Spiritual Attunement or Personal Growth groups have for a
great many people replaced going to church. Many people are deciding that they
are no longer interested in what the churches have to offer: "Everything You
Ever Wanted to Know About How to Live Every Facet of Your Life" in
prepackaged, convenient form.   More and more people have stopped believing in
a God who has dictated--via the clergy--a set of pat answers about conducting one's
life. Instead they are coming to conceive of a God who is within each
individual. Thus, group experiences that help individuals get in touch with their
inner selves are becoming increasingly popular: If God lives within oneself, then
to get in touch with one's own thoughts and feelings is also to get more in tune
with God.
I have participated in many, many groups through the years. They have gone
by many names: Personal Growth groups, Consciousness-Raising groups,
Therapy groups, Rap groups, Spiritual Attunement groups etc. Participating in

groups through the years has greatly enhanced my growth on a spiritual, emotional, and intellectual level. I have found that coming together with a group of other people to share insights provides me with the opportunity to glimpse reality in constantly new and exciting ways. By exchanging perceptions with other people, I am continually reaching a new understanding of myself and how I fit into this universe of which I am a part. Coming together with other human beings as equals, each sharing our deepest feelings, struggles, hopes, dreams, and fears, provides a wonderfully supportive and stimulating atmosphere in which I can explore the depths and heights of my humanness. Coming together to discover more fully the God that lies within each of us has been so much more rewarding to me than those stale church sermons I sat through for so many years. If the idea of putting together a group sounds interesting to you, I offer the following information which I hope will serve to assist you in starting a group.

Guidelines for Putting Together an Attunement / Affinity / Rap / Co-Counseling / Personal Growth / Consciousness-Raising / Group.

It is very important at the outset that a group make a lot of decisions about how it will operate, so that group members will not have incompatible expectations about the direction they want the group meetings to take. Though all groups may have similar over-all goals, such as helping each group participant more fully manifest his/her potential as a human being, there are an infinite variety of ways in which to go about such a task. It's important that the group clarify the specific means it wants to use to achieve its goals. On the following pages is a discussion of the various issues groups should decide on regarding group format.

STEP 1: **Deciding Whether the Group Will Have a Leader or Use Leaderless Format.**

A major decision a group must make is whether to have a leader or rotate group facilitation duties among group members. Through the years, I have participated in both groups which had a therapist as the group leader/facilitator and in leaderless groups. I will share my perspectives on the pros and cons of leader-facilitated vs. leaderless groups.

Let me start with the negative aspects of groups in which there is a leader. In some of the therapist-led groups I have participated in, I saw having a leader as being counter-productive to the group process. The therapists, by virtue of their position as group leader, became elevated to the position of "expert." In the way that members of the clergy are held in esteem as having some special "in" with God and knowing more about spiritual matters than the rest of us, I have seen therapists viewed as having a monopoly on the answers to happiness. Rather than finding their own answers through a discovery of the God within, group members continually looked to the therapist for answers. Such group experiences reinforce the idea of "experts" and hierarchical power structures.

On the other hand, I have been in groups in which a therapist served as leader, and I found these experiences very positive. The therapists were not into "power-tripping"; rather they maintained low-key roles as leaders and simply viewed themselves as catalysts, whose role was to help group members look into themselves and find their own answers. They operated under the philosophy that therapist Eric Berne popularized: The role of a good therapist is to work him or

18

herself out of a job as quickly as possible.

I have also had both negative and positive experiences through the years in leaderless groups. I had several experiences in leaderless groups, when I was younger, that were very negative and emotionally painful. There was no one in the group who had any group-process skills or knowledge and the group meetings would often turn into aimless and non-productive rambling. In addition, since none of the group members were very emotionally/spiritually healthy (myself included), there was a lot of game playing, destructive criticism, domination of some group members by others, and this sort of thing. Having had these negative experiences, I believe that a leaderless format is not always the best answer for any given group.

On the other hand, in the past few years I have participated in leaderless groups and the experience has been extremely positive. Most of the people in these groups had training in group process and had worked through their own psychological problems. Therefore, they did not inflict them on the group. It is such a beautiful experience to come together with a group of people and relate to them from a totally egalitarian position. I have found that when leaderless groups work, they are the most dynamic and growth-enhancing of all group experiences. I find leaderless groups particularly exciting because I view them as a microcosm in which to practice building a classless, non-hierarchical, egalitarian society. An excellent example of a successful leaderless group is The Quaker Society of Friends: The Quakers have held their weekly worship services with a rotating facilitator for hundreds of years.

In summary, I believe that personal growth groups function most optimally when the leadership/facilitation role is rotated among group members instead of designating one particular person, to serve as group leader or "therapist." However, since most people of my generation have been raised to deny our feelings; to be critical of ourselves and others; and in general to not be very emotionally healthy and balanced, we may presently need therapists to serve as group facilitators. However, I view therapist-facilitated groups as a transitional step towards a society in which therapist/client, group member/group leader are simply roles that each of us play at different times. I believe participating in therapist-led groups should enable group members to become capable of functioning as a therapist themselves. Hopefully some day in the future, the concept of therapists per se will appear to be a rather strange notion! Once we learn to raise children who are emotionally and spiritually healthy, there will be no need for therapists, all human relationships will be therapeutic.

If you are interested in increasing your group process skills there are a lot of very good books on the subject. Below is a list of books on group process. In order for a personal growth group to function optimally, it is important that all group members have training and skills in group process.

Book List For Developing Group Process Skills

(These books emphasize the leaderless or low-key facilitator group format.)

A Handbook for Consensus Decision Making--Building United Judgment, Center for Conflict Resolution, 731 State Street, Madison, Wisconsin 53703

Marshall Rosenberg, A Model for Non-violent Communication: A Manual for Group Facilitators, Center for Conflict Resolution, Madison, Wisconsin.

Peter Woodrow, <u>Clearness: Processes for Supporting Individuals and Groups in Decision Making</u>, Movement For A New Society, Philadelphia, 1978.

Bruce Kokopeli and George Lakey, <u>Leadership for Change; Toward a Feminist Model</u>, Movement For a New Society, Philadelphia, 1978.

Berit Lakey, <u>Meeting Facilitation: The No Magic Method</u>, Movement For A New Society, Philadelphia, 1975.

Auvine, Densmore, Extrom et. al., <u>A Manual For Group Facilitators,</u> Center For Conflict Resolution Madison, WI, 1977.

Coover, Deacon, et. al. <u>Resource Manual For a Living Revolution</u>, Movement For a New Society, Philadelphia, 1977

These books are textbooks for group therapists, however the information can be used to train any or all group members how to perform the group leadership functions.

Allen Ivey, <u>Intentional Interviewing and Counseling</u>, Brooks/Cole 1983

Gerald Corey, <u>Theory and Practice of Counseling and Psychotherapy</u>, Third Edition, Brooks/Cole, 1986 [There is an accompanying manual by the same name.]

Jeffrey Kottler and Robert W. Brown, <u>Introduction to Therapeutic Counseling</u>, Brooks/Cole, 1985

Joesph A. DeVito, <u>The Interpersonal Communication Book</u>, Harper & Row, 1986

Ronald Adler and Neil Towne, <u>Looking Out, Looking In</u>, 4th Edition, Holt, Rinehart & Winston, 1984

Napier and Gershenfeld, <u>Group Theory and Experience</u>, 3rd Edition, Houghton/Mifflin, 1985

Carl Rogers, <u>On Becoming a Person</u>, Houghton/Mifflin, 1961

Corsini and contributers, <u>Current Psychotherapies</u>, 3rd Edition, Itasea, Illinois, F.E. Peacock Inc., 1984.

William Cormier and L. Sherilyin Cormier, <u>Interviewing Strategies For Helpers</u>, Brooks/Cole/ 1985

Janet Moursund, <u>The Process of Counseling and Therapy</u>, Prentice Hall, 1985

Cavanaugh, <u>The Counseling Experience; A Theoretical and Practical Approach,</u> Brooks/Cole, 1982

Gerard Egan, <u>Face to Face; The Small Group Experience and Interpersonal Growth</u>, Brooks/Cole 1973

Irvin Yalom, <u>Encounter Groups; First Facts</u>, Basic Publishers, 1973

Howard Kirschenbaum and Barbara Glazer, <u>Developing Support Groups; A Manual For Facilitators And Participants</u>, University Associates, 1978

There is only so much that can be learned about group process from books, however. In order to develop good group process skills you must not only study group theory but get direct experience in a group. As I mentioned earlier I think that if groups are a new experience for you, it is best to start with a group that has a trained facilitator. You can then move on to the leaderless group format.

Step 2: Deciding on the Format of the Group Meetings

There are many different formats that personal growth groups can use. Let me discuss a few of the most common.

Discussion Topic Format

Groups that use the discussion topic format come together to explore a particular topic(s) in which they are mutually interested. Examples of this type of group would be divorced parents support groups, feminist-consciousness raising groups, and gay rap groups. Topic/discussion groups do not necessarily need to focus on one particular topic. In fact, some groups meet together and explore new topics every month or week.

There are an infinite number of discussion topics that work quite well in personal-growth or attunement groups. Here are some sample topics which have been popular in groups I have participated in through the years:

Relationship Topics

Do you prefer to be monogamous or polygamous? Share the reasons for your preference.

Do you consider yourself heterosexual, gay, or bi-sexual? Explain the reasons for your choice.

Do you consider life-long marriage the option most conducive to happiness? Why or why not?

Share your thoughts about the "secrets of staying in love."

Share difficulties in building a non-sexist relationship.

Have you ever chosen to remain sexually celibate for a given length of time? Why?

How do you cope with the end of a lover relationship?

How do you cope with the fear of AIDS? Has this disease made you less willing to have multiple sexual partners?

Human Problems Topics

Have you ever considered suicide? What made you decide to continue living?

How do you cope with the ever-present threat of nuclear destruction of the planet?

Share your insights about constructive ways to deal with anger.

Share three issues that you are feeling very confused about right now.

Share with the group a time in your life when you felt the most afraid and how you overcame your fear.

Religious/Philosophical Topics

Do you believe in a God? Share your perceptions of God.

Do you believe in an after life? What do you envision it to be like?

Do you believe in the concept of heaven and hell? Explain.

Do you believe in the concept of sin? Give five examples of what you would consider sins.

Do you belive there are two diametric forces--Good and Evil--operating in the universe? Explain.

Do you believe in reincarnation?

Reincarnational theories teach that in each lifetime the soul is incarnated to work through particular issues. What spiritual issues and challenges do you feel you are working on in this incarnation?

Most of the religions throughout history have spoken of the need to live a non-materialistic, "voluntary simplicity" lifestyle in order to find spiritual enlightenment. What are your thoughts on this?

Questions that generally help people get more in touch with who they are and where they are going with their lives are also excellent topics for groups. There are several popular modalities for these types of group exercises. One of the most popular is called "values clarification." "Values clarification" was developed by Louis Raths. The method was popularized the books <u>Values Clarification: A Handbook of Practical Strategies for Teachers and Students</u> and <u>Values Clarification for Counselors: How Counselors, Social Workers, Psychologists and Other Human Service Workers Can Use Available Techniques.</u> The concept is amazingly simple yet unbelievably effective. Here is a sample from the thousands of values clarification questions in these books:

If you had a million dollars to spend, how would you spend it?

If you had $10,000, how would you spend it?

If you had five years to live, how would you spend it? A week? A year?

List three goals you would like to accomplish in the next year, the next five, the next ten, the next twenty?

What do you consider the five greatest accomplishments of your life thus far?

Twenty things I love to do with my time are...

Do you want to have children? Why or why not?

Another popular modality used in personal-growth groups is called "sentence completion." This concept was invented and popularized by Dr. Nathaniel Branden in his books If You Could Hear What I Cannot Say and To See What I See And Know What I Know; A Guide to Self-Discovery. In sentence completion, group members share their answers to uncompleted sentences. Here are a few examples from the latter book.

As I learn to listen to my own inner signals...

As I look back over my life...

I see life as...

One of the things I want in a relationship and have never found is...

It's not easy for me to admit that...

If the child in me could speak he/she might say...

If I were willing to express my love more fully...

If I were fully comfortable with my sexuality...

The hard thing about being a man/woman is...

One of the ways I sometimes obstruct my own success is...

If I were to take full responsibility for my own existence...

If I were to allow myself to become more in touch with my own power...

As I become more sensitive to the things a deeper part of me knows...

Most groups rotate the task of thinking up an inspiring topic for the week among members. It's amazing to see all the interesting things people can find to talk to one another about!

23

Group Study Format

Groups that use this format are similar to a college seminar, except that there is no professor or leader. The group decides on a given list of books or articles to read and discuss together. I have participated in several such groups and found them very stimulating. Again there is an infinite number of books that would work for group study. Here are examples of some books that were used in groups in which I participated.

Jane Roberts, The Seth Material
Jane Roberts, Seth Speaks
Jane Roberts, The Nature of Personal Reality
Hermann Hesse, Siddhartha
Shirley MacLaine, Dancing in the Light
Shirley MacLaine, Out on a Limb
Helen Wambach, Life Before Life
Raymond Moody Jr., Life After Life
Kahlil Gibran, The Prophet
Fritjof Kapra, Tao of Physics
Richard Bach, Jonathan Livingston Seagull
Elisabeth Kubler-Ross, On Death and Dying
Stephine Levine, Who Dies
Robert Heinlein, Stranger in a Strange Land

James and Jongeward, Born to Win
Eric Berne, Games People Play
Eric Berne, What Do You Say After You Say Hello
Claude Steiner, Scripts People Live
Hugh Prather, Notes to Myself
Eric Fromm, Art of Loving
Sheldon Kopp, If You Meet the Buddha on the Road, Kill Him
Kenneth Keyes Jr., Handbook to Higher Consciousness
Carl Rogers, On Becoming a Person
Manuel Smith, When I Say No, I Feel Guilty
Leo Buscaglia, Love
Leo Buscaglia, Personhood
John Powell, Why Am I Afraid to Tell You Who I Am?
Carl Rogers, Becoming Partners
Nena and George O'Neill, Open Marriage
Anne Morrow Lindbergh, Gift from the Sea
Walt Whitman, Leaves of Grass

Marilyn Ferguson, Aquarian Conspiracy
B. Fuller, Critical Path
E. F. Schumacher, Small Is Beautiful
Frances Moore Lappe, Diet for a Small Planet
Frances Moore Lappe, Food First
Duane Elgin, Voluntary Simplicity
Adam Finnerty, No More Plastic Jesus
Simple Living Collective, Taking Charge
Michael Perelman, Farming for Profit in a Hungry World
Howard Zinn, A People's History of the United States

Boston Women's Health Collective, Our Bodies, Our Selves
Alice Walker, The Color Purple
Simone de Beauvoir, The Second Sex
Robin Morgan et al., Sisterhood Is Powerful
Betty Friedan, The Feminine Mystique
Starhawk, Dreaming the Dark
Robin Morgan et al., Sisterhood Is Global
Shalumith Firestone, Dialectic of Sex

Problem Sharing/Support Format

This format is more free-flowing. This would be the model used in therapy, counseling, or encounter groups. The group seeks to assist members in finding solutions/coping strategies to problems they are dealing with in their everyday lives. Groups using this format may use tools like role-playing, psychodrama, gestalt techniques, group massage, holding, rocking, etc.

Action Format

Groups working together on projects that are a manifestation of shared spiritual faith fall into this category. Some common examples would be groups that work to alleviate world hunger, peace activist groups, and groups which protest the production of nuclear plants, or destruction of the planet's ecosystem. Many of these groups meet together on a regular basis for support and spiritual attunement. The political activism of the group is thus an outgrowth of weekly group meetings. To give you a better sense of this type of group I have included a statement of purpose drafted by a group of peace activists. Calling themselves "Covenant For Peace", they are very active in peace political activism in the Detroit area.

We are unique human beings linked
with all of creation
And gathered from diverse places
to share a ministry of peace,
to challenge hopefully
to work for harmony and freedom.

We believe in an internal Source
an ever moving one.
Who creates and is creating
Who keeps covenant with humankind
Whose will for us is to choose life.

We believe in this creator's sustaining Presence
and transforming Power
Who dwells among us in clarity and mystery
Who inspires us individually and corporately
Who challenges, prods and emboldens.

We believe our believing affects
Our daily working and talking
Our decisions and choice making
Our responses to persons and systems.

We are people in the process of change.
We are moving, we are on our way.
We are seeking the promise of life and hope
   amid the symbols of our past and the experience
      of our present.
We seek wholeness--in our lives,
   in our relationships, in our community.
We seek--the sisterhood of man, the brotherhood
   of womanhood.
We want no part of power that is death-dealing,
   that dominates, oppresses and kills.
We want to participate in the power that is life
   supporting, that is
   grounded in the sense of human solidarity.
We are moving, we are on our way, we celebrate
   our struggle.

So in the midst of exploitation and oppression,
We dare this day to celebrate the power.
In the midst of despair and indifference,
We dare this day to celebrate the Hope.
In the midst of pain and violence
We dare this day to celebrate the Words.
In the midst of a machine-made society
We dare this day to celebrate the People.
In the midst of Fear, "national security"
   and the reality of death
We dare this day to celebrate the Life.
And we intend in these days
   to raise questions hopefully and
      to work for justice, peace, and freedom lovingly.

Covenant For Peace 1985
Reprinted with permission.

Your group may find after meeting together regularly for some time that you want to work on some projects together.

Step 3: Deciding On The Logistics Of The Group Meetings

The last but not least important step in forming a group is to decide on the little nitty-gritty things like how often you will meet, and where, and how many members to have in the group. Where a group meets is a very important consideration; particularly if you want group members to feel comfortable exploring their deepest feelings. The space provided must offer privacy so that if people want to scream or cry, they may do so out of earshot of people with whom they don't feel comfortable sharing such intense feelings. There's nothing like children or spouses or roommates interrupting a great group discussion to put a damper on it. It is also important that people be physically comfortable. Straight back chairs make it difficult to relax as do rooms that are too hot or cold or cluttered.

How often the group will meet is very important to decide at the outset. To some people, it is important that the group meet frequently, i.e., once a week. For other people whose lives are jammed with time commitments, monthly meetings work much better. Another important issue to discuss is how group members feel about people missing group meetings. Often groups like to agree that except for emergencies, people will try to make every session. Every person's presence comes to be valued in a group, and a person's energy and perspective is very much missed and noticed when he or she is not there. In groups where the discussion topics are less personal, the group may not feel a need to have a commitment from members to attend every meting.

The last consideration is group members should contract to meet for a given period of time. I would suggest that groups meet not less than six times and no more than 12 times. Then they should re-evaluate their objectives and allow each member to decide if he/she wants to re-contract or whether the group wants to recruit new members, or change its format. If this is not done, group members often feel pressured to continue with the group beyond the time that they really want to.

The optimum size for a group varies somewhat depending on what format the group is using. Groups that are operating on an intense emotional level should be small: five to eight members is considered the right amount for this type of group. Discussion groups that operate on a more intellectual level can function with more members: eight to fifteen is considered workable. Discussion groups that do not operate on an intense emotional level also tend to have greater absentee rates, so by having fifteen members, you may end up with only nine or so every meeting. Groups should periodically evaluate how they feel about the size of the group.

In summary, I firmly believe, from my own experiences in groups, that participating in groups is one of the best opportunities that exists for enhancing one's spiritual development. As I said earlier, if God resides within each of us, the more we come to know ourselves and one another, the more we come to know God. Meeting with other people in a group setting by whatever name is one of the best ways to better know and love both yourself and one another. Groups are the microcosm in which to practice manifesting all the ideals necessary to create the egalitarian, peaceful, and loving society which we all envision. Let me end this discussion of groups with this quote by the Bhagwan Rajneesh, in which he captures so beautifully the value of group interaction for spiritual development:

> *Life is in community. Life is a communion, so don't try to escape from the world, and don't try to remain in a solitary life. Because the richness is in the community; you are enriched by the community, by your relationships. The more you are related to people, the more you are rich. A solitary person living in a Himalayan cave is very poor, impoverished--because rivers of relationships don't flow inside him [or her]. He [she] becomes a desert.*
>
> *...Each time somebody looks into you, a river flows in. Each time somebody shakes a hand with you, an energy moves in you. When you drop out of all contacts, out of all relationship, and you become a solitary monk in a Himalayan cave, you have almost committed suicide. You are only one percent alive.*
>
> *When you don't want to relate with anybody, your contact with God is diminished, terribly diminished. When you come into relationship with another person, or with a tree, or with an animal, you are coming into contact with God in different*

forms. To be in community is the only way to be really alive. Relationship is life, and relationship is beautiful.

Just a few days ago a young man said to me, "I am meditating and great love is arising in me for humanity." I said, "For humanity"? How are you going to love humanity? Where will you find humanity? Humanity you say? Human beings will be enough. Love a human being, not humanity. "Humanity" is a trick of the head. Humanity? How will you love humanity? Where will you hug humanity? Where will you hold hands with humanity? You will always find a human being wherever you go; nowhere any humanity. Humanity is an ideology, a concept, an abstraction in the head. Life is always particular, the head is always conceptual. You will always find a certain human being, a man, a woman."

And when I said to the young man, "Love a human being," he was shocked. In fact, he was trying to escape into the "love humanity" to avoid human beings. No, he was not very happy when I said that. I could see in his eyes that he was not very happy--as if I had brought him down; he was flying very high. He was not flying at all; he was simply playing a verbal game.

If you love humanity, you can kill human beings to save humanity. If you love peace, you can go to war. Never love peace and never love democracy and never love communism --all ideologies.

Love concrete human beings, love concrete trees, love concrete rocks, particulars... only then will you know what love is.

Bhagwan Shree Rajneesh, <u>The Path Of Love,</u> Rajneesh Publications, 1978. Reprinted with permission.

Chapter 3

Alternative Marriage Rituals

The Need for Alternative Marriage Rituals

I became dissatisfied with the traditional marriage ritual of our culture after parting ways with Christianity. Traditional marriage rituals are heavily imbued with Christian values. Marriage is viewed as an irrevocable covenant between the couple and God: "Whom God has joined together, let no man put asunder." I had come to reject the idea of a God who dictated the specifics of one's lifestyle (see chapter 1). I no longer believed that God had decreed that lifelong marriage was the only spiritually correct lifestyle (second to celibacy, of course)! I therefore felt free to question whether the concept of lifelong marriage made sense to me based on my personal observations and experiences. In this chapter, I will outline the changes in belief I have undergone regarding marriage and, subsequently, marriage rituals. I hope that in doing so I can help other people who are unclear on their thoughts and feelings about marriage, lifelong and otherwise, to consider the issue in a new light.

For a number of years, even after I no longer considered myself a Christian, I still wondered if Christianity's premise that all marriages should be lifelong was, in fact, correct. I was an undergraduate student in psychology at the time, aspiring to be a clinical psychologist. Though psychology didn't preach that God had decreed that marriages were to be lifelong, the majority of psychologists were staunch supporters of lifelong marriage. Divorce was viewed as a manifestation of psychological problems. Thus, as a soon-to-be psychologist, I was trained to help couples with marital difficulties avoid divorce by helping them to overcome their psychological problems. All the psychologists I knew believed that "the alarming divorce problem in this country" could be solved by marital partners participating in therapy: therapy would improve the communication skills, mental stability, and overall emotional health of the marital partners, and they would as a result be able to maintain a happy, successful marriage.

Though I initially accepted the theories about divorce presented to me in my psychology curriculum, my personal experiences soon led me to have some doubts about their validity. As I began to interview divorcing/divorced couples I began to encounter more and more frequently couples whose divorces did not seem to be caused by any problematic behavior. These couples were as deeply committed and as emotionally healthy as any of the people I knew who had been married for thirty years. Yet these couples were led to conclude that they could no longer remain together happily as husband and wife.

As I continued to observe divorcing couples who didn't appear to have done anything wrong, I was led to an obvious question: if people weren't getting divorced (in many cases) because there was something wrong with them, could it be that something had gone wrong with the institution of marriage? Of course, I wasn't the only person asking that question. I experienced a tremendous sense of clarity as I allowed myself the freedom to ask not only what was wrong with people who couldn't make their marriages work, but also to ask what was wrong with the institution of marriage that people were no longer happy within it. I felt like the typical researcher who, after years of going in circles and finding no answers, suddenly discovers that he/she has been asking the wrong questions. I slowly began realizing that there were factors causing the divorce rate to spiral that could be described as environmental as opposed to personal.

One factor that definitely seemed to be playing a part in the spiraling divorce rate was the increase in human life-expectancy in the last hundred years. It is much less likely that two people will remain together happily from 18 to 80 than from 16 to 40. The longer people live, the more they grow and change, and the chances that they may grow in incompatible directions increases.

A second factor that seemed to be increasing divorce was the declining birth rate. Years ago people spent most of their married lives raising children. Though couples with children do divorce, it is complicated for them to do so. We are now seeing a lot marriages end when the partners are around the age of 45. By this time, the children are raised and the couple has no need to stay together "for the sake of the children." If the partners have grown in different directions they may no longer be very happy with one another and may choose to divorce.

Also affecting the divorce rate was the emergence of effective birth-control. Before sex could be separated from procreation, the idea of having several sexual partnerships throughout life would have meant having children with several partners. The complications inherent in this scenario made multiple marriages uncommon.

Another factor contributing to the increasing divorce rate was the large number of people turning away from Christianity. Many people besides myself were questioning the idea that lifelong marriage had been decreed by God to be the only acceptable lifestyle. New age religions were less rigid in the specifics of living and taught that spiritual enlightenment could be a part of a variety of lifestyles. Not to be ignored when analyzing why the divorce rate had increased was the simple fact that up until the last hundred years or so, people were so busy just subsisting that they had little time to examine the quality of their interpersonal relationships.

However, I came to believe that the most important factor in the increase of divorce was the women's liberation movement. Lifelong marriage, as an institution, evolved out of a social structure in which women were deprived of economic independence. Until women had a reasonable degree of economic independence, that is, access to jobs that paid more than subsistence wages, marriage was, for most women, not a choice but a necessity. For women, divorce meant going out into the world with no job skills and poor earning power. Under such circumstances, it was easier to remain with a spouse one didn't love than to face the poverty of single womanhood. A woman could trade one man for another, but of course that was no guarantee that the new marriage would be any happier. Men were also trapped by women's lack of independence. If a man no longer wanted to be married to his wife, he could not feel free to leave her without feeling guilty. Marriage was a woman's source of income and identity, and dissolving a marriage was to strip a woman of these necessities.

Though we are a long, long way from true equality between men and women, there have been dramatic improvements. Women, on the whole, have considerably more economic independence than they did before the women's liberation movement of the last twenty years. As a result of this economic freedom, women are much less likely to be forced to marry, or to stay married for economic reasons. Thus, more women are deciding that lifelong marriage is not the option most conducive to their happiness. Likewise, as a result of women's liberation, more men are deciding to end unhappy marriages, because they know their wives are no longer economically dependent on them and thus will not be devastated by divorce.

The women's liberation movement also increased the possibility of divorce because it increased the possibility that a husband's and wife's life paths would become incompatible. When women functioned as appendages to their husbands, without individual life goals or careers and with little encouragement to take into account their own personal needs, the question of whether or not a husband's and wife's life paths could remain compatible throughout their lives was a moot point. Women did not think of themselves as having lifetime objectives other than marriage and children. However, as a result of the women's liberation movement, marriage is now in many cases a joining of two growing, changing, evolving human beings, each with individual life goals, careers, and unique destinies to unfold. In such circumstances, it is far more likely that a husband and wife will grow and change in ways such that they can no longer remain husband and wife without stifling one another's growth and happiness.

I do not mean to imply that as soon as a woman becomes a feminist she will immediately file for divorce. I firmly believe that some people, staunch feminists included, may decide that lifelong marriage is the best choice for them. However, it does not take a very sophisticated social scientist to deduce from examining the divorce statistics of the last twenty years that there is a significant percentage of people who are deciding that lifelong marriage is not the best option for them.

The more I began to understand that a significant percentage of divorces were caused by environmental factors, not problematic behavior, the more my views about marriage and divorce changed. I realized that, in many cases, I could no longer label divorce as a "problem." Rather I began to think of divorce as a naturally occurring phenomenon with which many couples will have to cope. I became convinced that many marriages would not be lifelong and that this was not necessarily a bad thing. My experiences with divorced/divorcing couples led me to let go of the premise that the length of a marriage was always a measure of its success or failure. Instead I came to believe that the success of a relationship must be measured not in years, but in its ability to help partners grow and manifest their full potential as human beings.

After becoming convinced that in the coming years a significant percentage of marriages would end in divorce (because divorce was in many cases caused by environmental factors not likely to change), I became interested in designing a marriage ritual that did not contain an assumption that the marriage would be lifelong. I strongly believed that marriage rituals needed to be revised to incorporate the possibility of divorce for several reasons.

First, I was convinced after talking with many divorcing/divorced couples through the years that a great deal of the emotional pain and trauma people experience is caused by their ignorance about the possibility of divorce. The more I talked with divorcing/divorced couples, the more aware I became of their total shock and amazement when their marriages ended in divorce. I began to understand how much traditional marriage rituals contributed to this lack of preparation or knowledge about divorce by encouraging people to totally ignore its possibility. Inevitably, when two people stand on a marriage altar and publicly announce to all their friends and relatives that they promise always to love each other and to remain together forever, they are going to feel bitter, angry, and shocked when that doesn't happen. They are going to feel grossly disappointed and project their sense of failure on themselves and their partner. They may well have based many life/career decisions on the assumption of lifelong marriage, and they may feel resentful about missed opportunities and overwhelmed by the thought of picking up the pieces and going on with their lives. I thus came to believe that the denial of the possibility of divorce has a lot to do with why it is so emotionally devastating.

The second reason I was so interested in designing a marriage ritual that acknowledged the possibility of divorce was to improve the way in which divorcing couples deal with their children. Since traditional marriage rituals make the automatic assumption that the marriage will be lifelong, no forethought is given to how the children will be dealt with in the case of divorce. Most marital partners who have children together do not envision the possibility that they may someday be faced with the situation of parenting outside of their marital relationship. As a result of this lack of forethought divorcing parents often feel extremely angry and confused about how to deal with their relationships with their children. In addition, ex-spouses are sometimes so bitter about their divorces that they allow this bitterness to affect how they deal with their children. Quite often the father/child relationship is greatly diminished after divorce because the mother has negative feelings about her ex-husband. Divorced mothers often greatly limit the father's access to the children. In addition, when a divorced mother remarries, she often tries to make her new husband into a new father for the children, and tries to discourage the children from pursuing a close relationship with their biological father. The biological father's relationship is also sometimes greatly diminished because the mother decides to move across the country with a new spouse. Many divorced women make no attempt to coordinate their lives with the children's father so that he can continue to be near his children. The father/child relationship soon deteriorates to nothing more than a two week visit once a year and expensive long distance phone calls.

An equally sad situation often happens to the father/child relationship after divorce; the mother may want the father to continue his fathering role but he may refuse to have anything to do with the children. When this happens, the mother is placed in the difficult situation of trying to play both mother and father to her children. In addition, fathers too often cut off their financial support to their children after divorce. The family courts are full of cases of divorced mothers unsuccessfully trying to collect the child-support payments due them.

The fact that divorce has these extremely detrimental effects on parent/child relationships, and that it causes so much emotional pain and trauma to spouses in general, makes many people believe that marriage should be lifelong, and divorce avoided at all costs. However, I have come to believe it is possible for divorce to a) not be an emotionally devastating experience for spouses and b) not diminish the quality of the parent/child relationships. Let me outline how I came to this optimistic conclusion.

As I interviewed divorced/divorcing couples, I began to come in contact with more and more couples who were dealing with their divorce without feelings of bitterness towards one another and without jeopardizing either of the parent/child relationships. After discussing with these couples their amicable divorces and their success at maintaining close parent/child relationships after their divorces, I concluded that their success was due to their positive attitude about divorce. These couples were able to view divorce as the result of their growing and changing in ways that made it impossible to meet each other's needs. They did not view their divorces as having been caused by problems or inadequacies in themselves or their partners. As a result of this positive attitude, these couples were not bitter about their divorces, and in fact many of them maintained close friendships with one another. In addition, the couples did not view the end of their marriages as a barrier to their relationships with their children. These couples were able to mentally separate their relationships as lovers from their relationships as parenting partners. They continued to view their parenting partner relationships as lifelong commitments, despite the fact that their marriages had ended.

These couples were finding many creative ways to deal with parenting their children after divorce so that the children were able to have a close relationship with both mother and father. I met couples who were arranging for their children to live Monday through Friday with one parent and to spend the weekends with the other. I also encountered many divorced couples who purposely continued to live within a few miles of one another so that the children could continue to see each parent on a daily basis. I even met a few couples who had bought houses on the same block and one couple who shared a duplex! Despite the divorce, these couples displayed a strong commitment to continue to coordinate their lives so that each could continue to have a close relationship with their children.

The children in these situations did not seem in any way traumatized by the fact that their parents no longer lived together. In fact the parent/child relationships in these situations had actually improved as a result of divorce. The parents had felt so miserable and unhappy within their marriages that they had not been in a mental/emotional state to be very loving with their children. When these couples alleviated the source of their unhappiness--a marriage with irreconcilable differences--they became much happier individuals and, as a result, were able to be more loving and giving with their children.

Observing families who were dealing with divorce without apparent negative effects on the children made me come to the conclusion that divorce does not inherently diminish the quality of parent/child relationships; the negative effect that divorce often has on children is not a result of the parents no longer living together as husband and wife. The trauma stems from the parents' bitterness toward one another because of the divorce, and from their failure to arrange their lives so that each parent can continue to have a close relationship with the children.

I came to firmly believe that if marriage rituals were redesigned to incorporate the possibility of divorce, more couples would be able to deal with divorce in the positive way that the above described couples were dealing with it. I concluded that it is people's attitude toward divorce that makes it such a bitter and emotionally devastating experience. I also came to believe that if parents were encouraged to consider ahead of time that they might not remain married for as long as they would remain parents, they would be more mentally prepared and more committed to honoring their parenting commitments after divorce.

I do not intend to imply that divorce, even if acknowledged as a possibility before marriage, can be made painless. Transitions in relationships are always painful. However, for partners to remain in relationships where irreconcilable differences make it impossible for them to meet each other's needs is also painful for both them and their children. I also do not mean to imply that raising children as a divorced couple is an easy endeavor. People have repeatedly asked me "What happens if one parent gets a good job offer across the country and the other parent doesn't want to move?" "What happens if divorced parents don't want to coordinate their lives together?" These are very legitimate concerns. I always respond by saying, that if you know of any way to raise healthy, well-balanced kids without requiring any personal sacrifices on the part of the parents, let me know! I can only personally claim that I am willing to give up whatever freedom is necessary to coordinate my life with an ex-spouse because I think it is important for the children to have access to both parents. However, I am not willing to give up my freedom to terminate an unhappy marriage, because if I did, I would be so unhappy, that I could not parent well.

In summary, due to the many changes within our society brought on by such things as the women's liberation movement and increased life expectancy, a significant percentage of marriages will not be lifelong. Therefore, the traditional marriage ceremonies that assume "till death do us part" are ill-suited to the realities of people's lives. The need has arisen for marriage rituals that match the reality of people's lives in the late twentieth century.

I have therefore designed two marriage ceremonies which do not contain the assumption that the marriage will be lifelong. The ceremonies include a statement from each person acknowledging their inability to know how they as individuals may grow and change in the future. The partners also acknowledge that either of them has the right to terminate the relationship if he/she finds that his/her needs can no longer be met within it. The ceremony for people intending to have children together also contains a statement from each person promising to maintain their commitments as parenting partners even if they choose to terminate their relationship as lovers.

I believe these alternative marriage ceremonies will enable people whose marriages are not lifelong to deal with their potential divorces without bitterness and without the feelings of failure, inadequacy, and total confusion that are so common in divorce. I also hope that my proposed ceremony will help divorcing couples with children to realize that both mother and father can continue to have a close relationship with their children.

Some Logistical Considerations Regarding Alternative Marriage Ceremonies

Legal Marriage vs. "Non-legal Partnership"

If you decide to use the following alternative marriage ceremony (or your own alternative marriage ceremony), you will have to decide whether or not to have your ceremony legally recognized by the state. It is far beyond the scope of this book to deal comprehensively with the pros and cons of legal marriage as opposed to non-legal partnership. However, I would like to discuss the subject briefly.

We live in a society that strongly supports the institution of legal marriage and disapproves of sexual relationships (particularly where children are involved) that are not within the context of legal marriage. Thus, our social structure is set up to reward couples who are legally married and to punish those who defy the system. Non-legally married couples are often deprived of housing, jobs, social acceptance, and life and health insurance benefits, to name several problems. Certain income tax breaks require legal marriage, and non-legal partners are denied social security survivor benefits. In addition, certain rights to make legal decisions about your partner, e.g., medical decisions and funeral arrangements, are only granted to married couples. The list of advantages to married couples is very long. Considering the many factors working against non-married couples, one might logically ask why anyone would choose a non-legal partnership. Since I am one of those people who has chosen non-legal partnership, I will elaborate briefly my reasons for doing so.

Part of my decision to not legally marry stems from what you might call my anarchist tendencies. Something in me rebels against the idea of the state having control over my personal life beyond a very minimal degree. This discomfort escalated dramatically as I researched the legal ramifications of marriage. I discovered that family law allows very little room for the husband and wife to contract the kind of relationship they want.

Let me give you a few examples of things I learned about family law from my research. I was surprised to discover the degree to which husbands and wives are prohibited within marriage from contracting the terms of their financial arrangements. A husband, by family law, is required to support his wife, and a couple is not legally permitted to make any personal contracts to the contrary. That is, if a couple puts into writing that they will financially support themselves, or that the wife will support the husband, the court is permitted to overrule the contract if either spouse later becomes dissatisfied with the agreements he/she has contracted. Likewise, even if a husband and wife agree in writing that he will work at an outside job and pay her a certain amount for performing household work and childcare, the court can declare this contract null and void; a wife, by family law, is required to perform these services for free, as part of the marital contract. Another startling fact is that a wife can be divorced for desertion if she refuses to move where her husband wants to move, but the opposite is not true. In other words, the husband alone has the right to determine domicile.

From closely studying marital arrangements in family law, I learned that a marriage contract is not in reality a contract between husband and wife but instead a contract between the state and the wife, and the state and the husband. In short, the wife and husband have little say about the terms of the contract. Since we live in a sexist society, many of the conditions that the state includes in marriage contracts are thus quite often sexist. Last, but not least, the husband and wife do not even have the right, as with most contracts, to mutually agree to terminate "their" marital contract! Only the state can terminate it and decide on the terms of the dissolution. In sum, I felt that I was coerced into enough contracts with the state without willingly entering into another one. I opted for keeping my family relationships out of the legal system as much as possible, so that I could more freely contract with my partner about the kind of relationship we wanted to have with one another. If you would like to learn more about the legalities of marriage, I have found Lenore Weitzman's The Marriage Contract: Lovers, Spouses, and the Law to be the best book on the subject.

My second source of disagreement with legal marriage concerns the psychologically destructive effects I have repeatedly seen marriage cause. The concept of "getting married" implies that a couple's relationship is going to reach some fixed, unchanging state, when in fact relationships are flowing and ever-changing. I believe that were I to get married I would tend to think of my relationship in static terms; the very words imply a static state. I believe that "being married" would make me resistant to and afraid of the changes, ebbs and tides, and inherent unpredictabilities in human relationships.

To demonstrate this point, let me offer the example of the couple who marry and then divorce five or ten years later, instead of living together as non-married lovers for five years and then terminating their relationship. I have observed over and over again that the couples who legally marry and then divorce tend to look at their experience very differently from couples who do not marry. Couples who marry and subsequently divorce tend to use phrases like, "Our marriage didn't work". They often view their marriage as a mistake or failure, whereas the unmarried couple is more likely to view their five-year relationship with its parting of ways in a more positive, accepting way. The unmarried couple would not take the termination of their relationship as a sign that it didn't work. They would more likely speak in terms like this: "George and I met one another's mutual needs for five years. We both learned a lot, grew from the experience, and had a hell of a lot of fun together. However, we grew in very different directions and found that our life paths were no longer compatible. So we decided we would each be happier if we ended our relationship as lovers."

From my observations, when people get married, they make an assumption that their relationship should last for some specific length of time. In fact, since in the past marriage has always been associated with the concept of forever, I think it is difficult not to fall into thinking of it in that way subconsciously. I joke about marriage as breeding a "longer is better" attitude, and I see this as a detrimental premise. Participating in a legal marriage ceremony seems to cultivate in the couple the idea that by reciting marriage vows they have somehow created an unbreakable bond between themselves. When they later discover that the bonds that exists between lovers exist only as a result of the ability to meet each other's needs, and share compatible life goals and aspirations--and that this bond is not necessarily permanent--they find this very devastating and traumatic.

The concept of a marital bond tends to cloud the fact that the only permanent bond any of us has is to our own soul.   There needs to be room for our relationships with one another to change and flow as we move along whatever paths we are called to follow, to work toward our full potential as human beings and manifest our unique destiny. A given person may best be able to manifest his/her potential within the context of a fifty-year marriage. However, others might find that it may be most conducive to their happiness and growth to have five ten-year partnerships during the course of their lives. Thus, no matter how ecstatically happy and fulfilled my love relationship makes me in the coming years, I hope to fight the impulse to say, "Let's get married," because I sense that at some level I would be trying to capture, control, and put into a box love--the unpredictable and the uncontrollable.

To sum up my discussion of the pros and cons of legal marriage, I chose not to legally marry in order to make an important political statement: I felt it necessary to challenge the right of the state and the church to dictate the specifics of my own and other people's private lives. Though I am deprived of the many benefits that society offers legally married couples, I still believe that to marry would be the wrong choice for me: I would not want to subject myself to the negative psychological effects I have seen marriage have on people. In addition, by not succumbing to the social pressures to marry, I have been inspired to help work for reforms to restructure society's treatment of unmarried couples. For example, I have become active in protesting housing discrimination and have discovered a health insurance company that allows "significant others" to be declared as beneficiaries of health insurance.

However, to legally marry or not is a decision that each couple must make based on their unique values, needs and circumstances. For instance, some people may find that they can get legally married, and reap all the social benefits without marriage affecting them in psychologically negative ways. Perhaps some day I will decide it's worth it to get married on the basis of its social benefits, and I'll figure out how not to let being married affect me in a destructive way.

Public vs. Private Ceremonies

Another question you will have to consider if you choose to have an alternative marriage ceremony is whether or not to have a public ceremony or to have your marriage ritual be something you do privately. I will share briefly my ideas regarding private vs. public marriage ceremonies.

I personally make a distinction between couples intending to have children and those not intending to have children. I think it makes much more sense for commitments between non-parenting lovers to be expressed privately instead of publicly for the following reasons: I believe it will become more and more common for people to have several lovers in their lifetimes. I can envision it becoming rather common, for instance, for some people to have five ten-year relationships in their lifetimes as opposed to one forty-year relationship. It would not seem to make sense to have public ceremonies to designate these changes in lover relationships.

The second reason I do not believe it makes sense for non-parenting lovers to have a public ceremony to exchange vows is that, if people are not having children

36

together, they are always free to change or terminate their relationship. If they can freely terminate their relationship, then there is no need for them to make any irrevocable commitments. On the other hand, a parenting relationship demands certain commitments that are irrevocable; thus a public ceremony is more applicable. Secondly, parenting is, in a sense, a public matter because if a couple does not live up to their parenting commitments, society will have to take responsibility for the children. On the more positive side, the birth of a child is an addition to society. The community at large will be more affected by the birth of a child than by two people simply deciding to become lovers.

In general, becoming parents is a much more serious, difficult endeavor than deciding to become lovers. I think it can be very helpful for prospective parents to make public statements about their readiness for parenthood; to announce to the community their commitment to meet the supervisory and financial needs of their children; and to state their willingness to continue with their parenting commitments regardless of how their lover relationship changes. Having the community witness the commitments of prospective parents can enable family and friends to be a source of support for the parents in carrying out these goals.

I have therefore designed two alternative marriage ceremonies which are on the following pages. The first is called "Vows for Successful Lovers", and the second is called "A Parenting Partnership Ceremony". The lovers' vows are intended to be used when children are not involved, i.e., before a couple has decided to parent together or for couples not intending to have children. The lovers' vows are intended to occur privately as opposed to publicly. The parenting partnership ceremony is meant to be used at the time a couple is expecting their first child together. It is designed as a public ceremony.

Deciding On Names for the Partners and the Children:

It is an established tradition in our culture for women to assume their husband's names after marriage. However, women's rights advocates view this practice as oppressive to women and see it as an outgrowth of a social structure in which women are encouraged to give up their identities. Feminists have challenged the custom of women taking their husband's names since the 1800's:

> " . . .When a slave escapes from a Southern plantation, he [or she] at once takes a name as the first step in liberty--the assertion of individual identity. A woman's dignity is equally involved in a life-long name, to mark her individuality. We cannot overestimate the demoralizing effect on woman herself, to say nothing of society at large, for her to consent thus to merge her existence wholly in that of another."

> Elizabeth Cady Stanton, Proceedings of the Second Woman's Rights Convention, Rochester, New York, August 2, 1848, cited in Stanton, Anthony and Gage, History of Woman Suffrage, Vol. 1, p. 80.

As a result of the strong feminist movement of the last twenty years a significant number of couples have rejected the custom of the woman assuming the husband's name:

> "My husband and I see ourselves as two independent and equal people who have chosen to share our lives. Our relationship isn't one of homemaker and breadwinner, or protected and protector, but rather of two separate individuals who have in common certain interests and goals. Thus,

my becoming "Mrs. Him" would contradict not only the identities each of us has built up for him or herself, but also our definition of the relationship we have together."

Linda Roberson, Cited in <u>Booklet For Women Who Wish To Determine Their Own Names After Marriage</u>, Center For a Woman's Own Name, Barrington, IL., 1974.

One way that couples are dealing with the issue of names is for husbands and wives to hyphenate both of their names and use this as their new last name, for example, Maxwell-Ross. Though I appreciate this attempt at a non-sexist solution to names I personally think it is very inadequate for the following reason. It will not provide a solution to the other sexist custom regarding names in our culture: naming all the offspring of a marital union the father's surname. If couples hyphenate their names and use this as a surname, the second generation is going to be in big trouble. What happens when Mary Maxwell-Ross marries another child of a liberated marriage George Brown-Beechwood? Thus, hyphenated names are not feasible beyond one generation.

One possible way to deal with the issue of names for partners and children is for both partners to retain their own names after marriage and to name all the female offspring with the mother's surname and all the male offspring with the father's surname. This is at least a workable solution. However, I have come up with what I think is an even better solution to the dilemma of names.

My partner and I have decided to give each of our children his/her own individual name first, middle and last. I came up with this idea one day when I was thinking about the fact that Native Americans do not pass surnames to their children. Every Native American child is given his/her own, unique name at birth and retains this name throughout his/her life. Thus, there are no Tom or Nancy Sitting Bull's nor any Black Elk Juniors! The idea of children having their own names made a lot of sense to me: I didn't want to view my children as appendages to myself any more than I thought women should be viewed as appendages to their husbands.

My partner and I have been given some negative feedback about our idea of giving all of our children their own names. People have told us that our children will be traumatized that they do not have the same names as their parents or their siblings. I find this reasoning ridiculous in light of the number of children that have different names than their parents or siblings due to divorce and remarriage; it is not as unusual a phenomenon as some people make it out to be. We are excited about making up meaningful names for our children. Thus, as we look through baby name books we also look for names that we could use for a surname, names that have a nice meaning. Some examples are: Alexander--helper of humankind, Roland--adventurous, or Woodward--keeper of the forest.

Every couple must, of course, make their own decisions as to what to do about their own names after marriage, and how they will deal with naming their children. I present these ideas as suggestions--every couple must decide on an option that they feel comfortable with. What's most important is that people feel free to <u>question</u> customs regarding names so that they can make their own decisions about what names they will use for themselves after marriage and what names they will give their children. I recommend that couples announce at their "marriage" ceremonies what they have decided to do regarding their names. This will help alleviate the problems some couples encounter when friends and relatives automatically assume that the women will be taking the husband's name.

The Ceremonies...

Vows For Successful Lovers

A Parenting Partnership Ceremony

Introduction to Vows for Successful Lovers

This ceremony is designed to be used by couples when children are not involved, that is, before a couple has decided to parent together, or for couples not intending to have children. As I mentioned earlier in this chapter, I do not envision these vows being recited in a public ceremony. Rather I see them as being exchanged privately between the couple. I have friends who have designed their own vows and recited them to each other on a mountain top. I like this idea. Couples might even consider reciting their relationship vows each year on their anniversary, with any revisions they would like to make.

Let me also say a few words about the content of the ceremony. I chose to call this ceremony "Vows For Successful Lovers" so a definition of a successful relationship is called for. I define a successful lover relationship to be one which:

a) is satisfying to both people on an emotional, intellectual, and spiritual level.

b) enables both people to continually grow and more fully manifest their potential as human beings.

c) contains the wonderful elements of fun, excitement, and passion.

These vows are my attempt to put into a tangible, workable format the elements I have come to believe enhance a couple's ability to achieve such a relationship. It is, of course, only a tool; reciting these vows will not magically make a couple's relationship work. It is my hope, however, that the words can be a framework to work from. I hope it can be returned to for inspiration and guidance in those turbulent, difficult times experienced in any relationship.

You will note that these vows contain options regarding monogamy: the couple may choose to exchange pledges to remain sexually monogamous or they may grant one another freedom to explore other sexual relationships. Having interviewed many, many couples over the years, I have come to believe that monogamy is a matter of preference, and should not be considered an automatic requirement for every lover relationship.

These vows are also meant to be supplemented with a written contract. The written contract should be a legal document that deals, in more detail, with the logistics of the relationship. Two excellent books on how to write contracts for both marital and non-marital relationships are Lenore Weitzman's The Marriage Contract: Lovers, Spouses, And The Law, and Toni Ihara and Ralph Warner's The Living Together Kit.

Lastly, I need to state, as I have throughout this book, that these vows are meant as an example. I hope they can serve as a catalyst to help couples write their own vows, specifically suited to their needs and values.

Vows For Successful Lovers

Person #1:

I love you. Being with you enhances my life and brings me the greatest joy. When I am with you I feel content and peaceful and vibrantly alive. When I look into your eyes or hold you in my arms, our souls reach out to each other and I feel a warmth in the depth of my being. You are a comfort to me in times of sadness, and it is with you that I want to celebrate the triumphs of my life.

Person #2:

I love you. Sharing my life with you sustains and enriches me. There exists between us a very deep emotional, intellectual, and spiritual bond. You are my companion in our separate but intertwined pathways of growth. Each day you help me to become a more full human being.

Person #1:

In order that our love may grow and that our relationship be all it can be, I make the following pledges.

Person #2:

So as to nurture the love we share, I make the following pledges.

Person #1:

I pledge honesty to you. Not only do I promise not to purposely deceive you, but I promise not to lie to myself and repress the truth because it may be painful. I promise to do all I can to be in touch with myself and to share anything with you that I believe you would want or need to know.

Person #2:

I pledge this to you also.

Person #2:

I promise to not stop myself from taking risks in relating to you because I am fearful. To do so would be to prohibit any chance for improvement and to settle for less than we could be.

Person #1:

I pledge this to you also.

Person #1:

I promise to truly listen to you, to strive to the best of my ability to understand what you are thinking and feeling. I promise to give you feedback so that you may understand yourself better.

Person #2:

I pledge this to you also.

Person #2:

I promise not to be critical in a destructive way. I promise to not belittle your efforts, knowing that you are doing the best you are capable of at the time.

Person #1:

I also promise this to you.

Person #1:

I promise to be patient. I promise to give you the space and time you need to work things through at your own pace, and not to push you.

Person #2:

I pledge this to you also.

Option #1

Person #1:

I pledge to be monogamous with you. Though I know I will at times feel sexually attracted to other people, I choose to make a commitment not to act on those feelings. I want to focus my energy on this relationship, because I believe that to be sexually intimate with more than one person leads to feelings of fragmentation. Only when I give myself wholly to one person am I able to reach and maintain that special, deep, intense level of intimacy. I also choose to be monogamous so that I have more time and energy for friends, myself, my family, my work, and for my community involvement.

Person #2:

I also pledge to be monogamous with you. I have found that only within a one-to-one relationship can I feel safe enough to open the deepest levels of myself and achieve full intimacy. I know I will sometimes feel sexually attracted to other people, but I choose not to act on those feelings. Sexuality demands an intense commitment of emotional energy, and my time and energy commitments with you would not allow me to adequately meet the emotional needs of another sexual relationship. I also choose to be monogamous so that I have more time for friends, family, myself, my work and for community involvement.

Option #2

Person #1:

I pledge to allow you the freedom that you may need through the course of our relationship to explore love relationships with other people. I realize I cannot meet all of your needs, nor you all of mine. I believe that each of us will grow and be enriched by experiencing love with other people, and that to limit one another's freedom would be stifling and stagnating to our relationship.

Person #2:

I also pledge to allow you the freedom that you may need through the course of our relationship to explore love relationships with other people. I believe there sometimes will be needs that we cannot meet in one another. I believe that by allowing one another to get those needs met in other relationships, we can better enjoy the unique gifts that we give to one another.

Person #1:

I pledge a commitment to my own personal growth because when I grow, my growth enriches the relationship, and when I allow myself to stagnate, that stagnation permeates the relationship.

Person #2:

I also promise this to you.

Person #2:

I pledge to acknowledge at all times that each of us has needs to be considered and respected and I pledge to search for creative solutions to conflicts and workable compromises.

Person #1:

I also promise this to you.

Person #2:

I promise not to run or give up when relating becomes difficult, knowing that relationships, like life, have their rough spots. I promise to take time to find out if the problems can be solved before terminating the relationship.

Person #1:

I also promise this to you.

Person #1:

I promise to remember that as much as we now love each other, we cannot predict that we will always love each other as we do today, or that we will want to remain together for the rest of our lives. I acknowledge that we are both growing, changing people and that as a result of our on-going life experiences we may become unable to continue to meet each other's needs as lovers. I promise to remember that each of us must manifest our destiny as individuals, and that we may not always be able to do that within the context of our lover relationship.

Person #2:

I, too, promise to remember that as much as we now love each other, we cannot know how we as people may grow and change in the future. I pledge to remember that the words "I love you" are always a statement of fact, not a promise. I promise to remember that we may someday find that our life paths are no longer compatible.

Person #1:

If we should find that we can no longer meet each other's needs, I pledge to participate in a termination process. I promise to share with you, to the best of my ability, why I believe the relationship is no longer meeting my needs.

Person #2:

I pledge this to you also.

Person #2:

If we choose to terminate our relationship as lovers, I promise to remember that the length of a relationship is not a measure of its success or failure. I promise to measure the success of our relationship by the extent to which it helped each of us to grow towards our fullest potential as human beings.

Person #1:

I also promise this to you.

Person #1:

   If we choose to end our relationship as lovers, I promise to accept the pain of that ending as growing pains, and to look back with an appreciative joy at all we received from one another.

Person #2:

   I also promise this to you.

(Pause)

Person #2:

   I commit myself to nurturing our love to the best of my abilities. I will strive each day to make our relationship a source of common energy from which each of us can draw the strength and courage to become all that we can be. May we each day touch souls in a new way and become more whole.

Person #1:

   I commit myself to nurturing our love to the best of my abilities. I will strive each day to make our relationship a vehicle for the personal evolution of each of us. I rejoice in the love we share.

Introduction to the Parenting Partnership Ceremony

I envision this ceremony taking place during approximately the third month of pregnancy. I choose that time because there are a great number of people who discover they are infertile. Thus, I don't think it's a good idea for a couple to have a ceremony to become parenting partners until they know in fact that they can have a child. This will avoid a lot of disappointment. There are, of course, a percentage of people whose pregnancies will not come to term. Yet I still think having this ceremony in the third month of pregnancy makes sense, because it provides the large percentage of couples whose pregnancies will be successful, with the opportunity to have six months to mull over all the commitments they have made and to prepare themselves to carry them out.

As I mentioned earlier in this chapter, this is meant to be a public ceremony. You will note that there is no facilitator. The couple "marries" themselves instead of being married by a representative of the State or the Church. As I have suggested throughout this book, I do not think we need religious or political authority figures to perform our rituals for us. I find this concept elitist, oppressive, and stifling. Perhaps as an alternative the couple may want a few friends to read poems, sing songs, or bless the union to enhance the ceremony.

The vows from "Vows for Successful Lovers" are included as part of this ceremony, since a good many of the commitments necessary in a lover relationship are, of course, also applicable in a parenting partnership. However, there are many additional commitments that parenting partners need to make; therefore, this ritual has additional vows relating to parenthood. It is possible that the couple may have recited the lover's vows previously, but I think it's important to re-state them as part of this ceremony.

These parenting partnership vows, like the lovers' vows, contain options for the couple to either agree to be monogamous or to agree to have a sexually open marriage. I don't believe it should be assumed that when people become parents, this automatically means that they should from then on be monogamous. I know from watching my friends who are parents, that parents have a lot less free time and energy, and thus will not be able to have as many outside relationships as they might have had before the children. However, to the extent that time and energy allow, some couples may want to maintain their freedom to relate sexually outside of their relationship.

There are several other important components of this ceremony that are not included in traditional marriage ceremonies. This ceremony includes a statement from partners acknowledging that they are both growing, changing people and thus cannot predict if their marriage will be life-long. Both people also state that they will continue to honor their parenting commitments even if they terminate their relationship as lovers. A very important part of this ritual, which is not a part of traditional marriage ceremonies, is the couple's commitment to their unborn child, about the kind of parents they aspire to be. I think this concept addresses a very important lack in traditional marriage ceremonies. Parenting is one of the most difficult endeavors we as human beings encounter in our lives. Yet we have no ritual that prepares people for the difficult task of parenthood. I admit that making pledges in a parenting ceremony is certainly not instant certification that a couple will make good parents. However, I think it is at least a beginning, a step in the right direction.

This ceremony also contains a pledge from both mother and father to share equally the financial and supervisory care of the children. Unfortunately, this pledge is not legally binding. Whatever laws are in effect in a given state regarding a mother's and father's responsibility for financial and supervisory care of their children will override any contrary pledges of the parents. The state has the authority to decide which parent gets custody, and how much financial support the non-custodial parent must pay the custodial parent for child-support. However, I have included this pledge by the parents because it is what I consider to be the ideal. Perhaps in a few decades women will have equal earning power to men, and men will be more involved in direct child-care, and the child-support laws will be revamped so as to delegate equal responsibility to mother and father for financial and supervisory care of the children.

In the meantime, it is up to couples to individually create this equal sharing, through their own personal agreements. It is my hope that couples will honor the agreements they make with one another regarding all facets of child-raising. Obviously however, there is a risk that either parent will renege on their agreements with one another and subsequently the state will be called in to decide who provides what, in terms of both financial support and supervisory care.

Though parents may not be able to make legal contracts regarding the specifics of their child-support arrangements, they can make legal agreements about other aspects of their relationship, particularly if they do not legally marry. Thus, this parenting partnership ceremony is meant to be supplemented with a written, legal contract. The written contract should deal with the many logistical aspects of the relationship not appropriate to recite publicly, but nevertheless extremely important. Two excellent books on how to write contracts for both marital and non-marital lover relationships are Lenore Weitzman's The Marriage Contract: Lovers, Spouses, and the Law and Toni Ihara and Ralph Warner's The Living Together Kit.

Lastly, I would like to state that this ritual is meant only as an example, to be used as food for thought. Obviously, if I were to insist that all couples use this specific ritual, I would be acting as dogmatically as the churches. I believe each couple should write their own parenting partnership ceremony unique to their needs. Perhaps there are components that should be included in all parenting partnership rituals, e.g., a pledge to honesty and a pledge to honor one's parenting commitments even if the lover relationship ends. But ultimately there is lots of room for individuality.

A Parenting Partnership Ceremony

Woman:

Family and friends, we ask you to share in celebration with us as we proclaim our love and commitments to each other. We will soon share one of the greatest of all human experiences--having a child. In order that we may prepare ourselves for this new role, we want to take this time to define our expectations, needs, and goals, so we will be ready for our new relationship as a family.

Man:

We have asked your presence today because we hope that by sharing our goals and commitments with you, that you can be a source of support for us in carrying out these dreams and goals. Likewise we hope we can help all of you in the daily process of your lives and struggles. We believe that families are enriched when they are bonded together to form community.

Man and Woman:

Please rejoice with us as we proclaim our love.

(Pause)

Woman:

I love you. We share the same dreams, aspirations, and vision of the world. Being with you enhances my life and brings me the greatest amount of joy I have ever known. When I am with you I feel content and peaceful and vibrantly alive. It is you I can turn to for comfort in moments of despair, and it is with you that I want to share the triumphs of my life.

Man:

I love you. Sharing my life with you sustains and enriches me. You bring a warmth to the depth of my soul. There exists between us a bond so strong that I feel as though I have known you for lifetime upon lifetime. Our relationship serves as a vehicle for the personal evolution of each of us, each day we help one other to become more full human beings.

Woman:

So as to nurture the love we share, I make the following pledges.

Man:

In order that our love may grow and our relationship be all that it can be, I make the following pledges.

Woman:

I pledge honesty to you. Not only do I promise not to purposely deceive you, but I promise not to lie to myself and repress the truth because it may be painful. I promise to do all that I can to be in touch with myself and to share anything with you that I believe you want or need to know.

47

Man:

I also pledge these things to you.

Man:

I promise to not stop myself from taking risks in relating to you because I am fearful. To do so would be to prohibit any chance for improvement and to settle for less than we could be.

Woman:

I pledge this to you also.

Woman:

I pledge a commitment to my own personal growth because when I grow, my growth enriches the relationship, and when I allow myself to stagnate that stagnation permeates the relationship.

Man:

I also promise this to you.

Option #1

Man:

I pledge to be monogamous with you. I know I will at times feel sexually attracted to other people. However, I choose to make a commitment to not act on those feelings, because I want to focus my energy on this relationship. I have found to be sexually intimate with more than one person leads to feelings of fragmentation. Only when I give myself wholly to one person am I able to reach and maintain that special, deep level of intimacy. I also chose to be monogamous so that I have more time and energy for friends, myself, my family, my work, and for community involvement.

Woman:

I also pledge to be monogamous with you. For I have found only within a one to one relationship can I feel safe enough to open the deepest levels of myself and achieve full intimacy. I know I will sometimes feel sexually attracted to other people but I choose not to act on those feelings. My time and energy commitments with you would not allow me to adequately meet the emotional needs of another sexual relationship. I also choose to be monogamous so that I have more time and energy for my friends, family, myself, my work, and for community involvement.

Option #2

Man:

I pledge to allow you the freedom that you may need to explore love relationships with other people. I realize I cannot meet all of your needs nor you all of mine. I believe each of us will grow and be enriched by experiencing love with other people, and that to limit one another's freedom would be stifling and stagnating to our relationship.

Woman:

I also pledge to allow you the freedom that you may need, to explore love relationships with other people. I believe there will sometimes be needs that we cannot meet for one another. I believe that by allowing one another to get those needs met in other relationships, that we can better enjoy the unique gifts we give to one another.

Man:

I pledge to acknowledge at all times that each of us has needs to be considered and respected and to search for creative solutions to conflicts and workable compromises.

Woman:

I also promise this to you.

Woman:

I promise to listen to you, to strive to the best of my ability to understand what you are thinking and feeling. I promise to give you feedback so that you may understand yourself better.

Man:

I pledge this to you also.

Man:

I promise not to be critical in a destructive way. I promise to not belittle your efforts, knowing that you are doing the best you are capable of at the time.

Woman:

I also promise this to you.

Woman:

I promise to be patient. I promise to give you the space and time you need to work things through at your own pace, and not to push you.

Man:

I pledge this to you also.

(Pause)

Woman:

We would now like to declare our readiness for parenthood.

Man:

We know that in becoming parents we will be pushed to achieve the fullest heights of our humanness. For in order to parent successfully, we must become more capable of unconditional love, of forgiveness, of compassion. As parents, we know we must learn to give freely, without thought of what we shall receive in return.

Woman:

Yet in such giving, we know we shall experience the miraculous wonder of giving becoming, in itself, receiving, as we recognize that only by giving of ourselves to others do we become fully human.

Man:

As we nurture and love our children, we know that we shall be enriched. Our lives will take on new meaning as we see ourselves as an integral link in the ever-evolving family of all people. In becoming parents we shall become instruments of the creative energy of the universe, through which is born new life. We will become, as Gibran says, "A bow from which children as living arrows are sent forth upon the path of the infinite."

(Pause)

Woman:

In order that I may become more the mother I aspire to be, I make the following pledges.

Man:

In order that I may become more the father I aspire to be, I make the following pledges.

Woman:

"I know I must alter my life in order to meet the needs of this fragile being that will soon be entrusted into our keeping. I know I must learn to give, learn to put the needs of another before my own. I know that I must give up certain freedoms. I feel ready to give up these freedoms because I have done the things I needed and wanted to do with my life that wouldn't have been possible with a child. I will therefore not view having a child as having prohibited me from living my life as I wanted. I have a solid sense of who I am and what paths I want to take with my life. I therefore believe I have energy to focus on helping a child find his/her answers to these questions. I know being a parent requires a tremendous amount of giving, however, I believe watching our children grow and blossom will be repayment a thousand-fold for the giving I will do.

Man:

I know there are certain freedoms I have always had which I must let go of in order to be a source of strength and stability from which our children can draw. I have waited until now to become a father so that I would be ready to give up these freedoms freely, without regret. I have accomplished the things I needed to accomplish before I could be ready to devote the necessary time and energy into meeting the needs of a child. I have an understanding and sense of who I am and what paths I want to take with my life. I am ready to put the needs of a child before my own. I believe that the joys of participating in the growth and unfoldment of our children will be, if anything, an overpayment for the giving I will do.

Woman:

We believe that in order to provide our children with the stable mothering and fathering relationships they need, we must view the parenting commitments we make today as a life-long endeavor. Yet, we know that we cannot guarantee that our relationship as lovers will last for a lifetime.

Man:

We recognize that we are both growing, changing people, and that as a result of our on-going life experiences, we will change in ways which we cannot predict. We acknowledge that we may someday find we can no longer remain lovers without stifling one another's growth and happiness. Therefore, we know that we must be willing to honor our parenting commitments, even if we have chosen to terminate our relationship as lovers. We therefore make the following pledges.

Woman:

I pledge that regardless of how our relationship as lovers may change in the future, these changes will not alter the parenting commitments I make today. I accept our relationship as parenting partners as a life-long commitment. We are and will always be a family, connected and bonded together by our biological links. Regardless of how our lover relationship changes in the future, I am committed to coordinating my life with yours so as to allow each of us to have a close, on-going relationship with our children.

Man:

I hereby pledge that however our relationship as lovers may change in the future, these changes will not alter the parenting commitments I make today. You will always be the mother of my children. Our relationship as parenting partners is a life-long relationship. If we someday choose not to live together as lovers, I am committed to setting up a new living situation that allows each of us to continue to be a integral part of our children's lives.

Woman:

We recognize that in order for our children to be able to have a close, on-going relationship with each of us, it is important that we always treat each other with respect and compassion.

Man:

We are committed, therefore, regardless of whether or not we remain lovers, to always respect one another's right to teach our children our values and ideas, though we may at times disagree with one another.

Woman:

We would like to end our ceremony by making pledges to our children to be.

Man:

In order to parent successfully, we believe we must manifest the wisdom the poet Gibran captured in his moving poem "On Children."

Woman:

We would now like to read the poem "On Children" from Kahlil Gibran's book The Prophet.

Woman:

> *Your children are not your children.*
> *They are the sons and daughters of Life's*
> *longing for itself.*
> *They come through you but not from*
> *you,*
> *And though they are with you yet they*
> *belong not to you.*
>
> *You may give them your love but not*
> *your thoughts,*
> *For they have their own thoughts.*
> *You may house their bodies but not*
> *their souls,*
> *For their souls dwell in the house of to-*
> *morrow which you cannot visit, not even*
> *in your dreams.*

51

Man:

> *You may strive to be like them, but seek*
> *not to make them like you*
>   *For life goes not backward nor tarries*
> *with yesterday.*
>   *You are the bows from which your children*
> *as living arrows are sent forth.*
>   *The archer sees the mark upon the path*
> *of the infinite, and He bends you with His*
> *might that His arrows may go swift and far.*
>   *Let your bending in the archer's hand*
> *be for gladness;*
>   *For even as He loves the arrow that flies,*
> *so He loves the bow that is stable.*

(Pause)

Man:

In order to be the parents we aspire to be, we make the following pledges.

Woman:

My children to be, I pledge to the best of my abilities to understand and meet your needs and to help you find the things in life that are not mine to give.

Man:

My children to be, I pledge to the best of my abilities to understand and meet your needs, and to help you find the things in life that are not mine to give.

Woman:

My children to be, we pledge to appreciate the beauty and uniqueness of you and to remember that you are not in this world to live up to our expectations, but to manifest your own personal destiny.

Man:

My children to be, in helping you find answers and make decisions, we pledge to give you advice from your frame of reference, in accordance with your values and needs, not our own. We pledge to remember that reality is constantly changing, and, therefore, the behaviors and values that were right for us in our lives may not be right for you in yours.

Woman:

We promise to protect you from danger, yet at the same time to remember that it is not our job to protect you from all risks. We must learn to not let our fears for your safety stop you from taking the risks you need to take in order to grow and do what you need to do with your life.

Man:

We promise patience. We promise to give you the space and time to work things through at your own pace, and not to push you. We promise not to be critical in a destructive way, respecting your right to make mistakes.

Woman:

My children to be, we want to teach you to listen to others for all that they can teach you, and also how to turn inward for the answers that lie within yourself.

Man:

We want to help you experience life as beautiful--to see the beauty in all people and all things and to interact with the world with caring and respect.

Woman:

We promise to remember to continue to get our own needs met, because when people feel good inside, their love flows out of them to those around them, and when they feel empty, they have nothing to give. We promise to remember that to love others, we must first love ourselves.

Man:

My children to be, we know we will be bringing you into a world filled with much pain and confusion. We are bringing you into a world that teeters on the brink of annihilation. We are often filled with sadness and grief at the injustice of this world and know that you, too, will have to cope with much pain here. Yet we choose to bring you into this world because we believe in the existence of the soul, which transcends this physical existence. As difficult as this life is at times, we believe that there is a purpose for what happens to us here. We have faith that we are all here to learn lessons that we can learn in no other way. We believe that living on this planet through these painful and difficult times will provide you with life experiences which are necessary for the enlightenment of your spirit.

Woman:

My children to be, we rejoice at the thought of your birth. We know you shall enrich our lives as we struggle together through the sometimes slow and painful, but also joyous and exciting, process of growth. We look forward to helping each other in working toward the fullest heights of our humanness.

Man:

Family and friends, will you now witness as we solemnize our partnership?

(Pause)

Woman:

I want you as my parenting partner because we share many of the same dreams, aspirations, and visions of the world. Though I understand all children must ultimately define their own version of truth, I know that our children will turn to us for answers, guidance, and knowledge for many years. I am confident about the answers you will give, because I believe that they will match closely my own, though maybe not in specifics, in spirit. I have also chosen you because the constant love, nurturing, and support you have given me makes me confident that our child will never lack for any of these.

(Pause)

I hereby take you as my parenting partner. I promise to nurture you, give you of my strength in times of need, celebrate your joys and triumphs, and care for you in sickness. I pledge to share equally with you the financial and supervisory care of our children.

Man:

I want you as my parenting partner because I trust the ways in which you will mold the souls of our children. I understand that we can never know what course our children will choose to take with their lives. Yet I also know that what children learn and receive from their parents has much to do with what they will become, and I trust in you. I have also chosen you because of your patience and caring.

(Pause)

I hereby take you as my parenting partner. I promise to nurture you, give you of my strength in times of need, celebrate your joys and triumphs, and care for you in sickness. I pledge to share equally with you the financial and supervisory care of our children.

(Pause)

Woman:

We thank you for sharing this important occasion in our lives with us.

Man:

We thank you for witnessing our vows and sharing in our joy.

54

Chapter 4

Alternative Funeral Rituals

Introduction

I became interested in designing an alternative funeral ritual because the funeral rituals I have participated in throughout my life have left me feeling extremely frustrated, dissatisfied, and alienated. I have found the traditional funeral rituals in our culture to be pious, ostentatious, and laden with social and religious values that are in total contradiction to my own. The purpose of a funeral ritual is to make the very painful experience of death less painful. However, I found that traditional funeral rituals thwarted rather than helped my grieving process. From talking with many, many people about funerals I realized that most people's experiences of funerals had been as negative as my own. Therefore, I came to believe that there was a very urgent need for alternative funeral rituals. I felt called upon to tackle this challenging endeavor.

Designing an alternative funeral ritual was much more complex and difficult than writing any of the other rituals in this book. The first factor which makes designing an alternative funeral difficult are the many legal restrictions that exist regarding funeral practices in this country. For example, though I might personally wish for my surviving family to set up a funeral pyre out in the woods behind my house and cremate my body, that unfortunately is <u>not</u> an option. So in order to design an alternative funeral, I first had to familiarize myself with many laws to ensure that my alternative rituals could in fact be carried out.

The second factor that made designing an alternative funeral ritual difficult was that death rituals in any culture tend to be viewed as sacred. Therefore, anyone who attempts to question funeral rituals will be strongly discouraged from doing so and will receive an enormous amount of criticism. I initially found this discouragement and criticism very difficult to deal with.

Another factor contributing to the difficulty of designing an alternative funeral was that it forced me to resolve, within myself, a great many philosophical issues. I found that I had to sort out my conflicting thoughts and feelings about God, afterlife, Heaven and Hell, reincarnation and so forth. Like most people, I had found it easier to put off thinking about these issues, but I had to tackle them if I wanted to write an alternative funeral ritual.*

---

*Obviously my beliefs about God, afterlife. etc. will continue to change throughout the years. Thus, I do not mean to imply that it is possible to resolve these issues permanently. However, I needed for the purpose of writing this chapter, to "take a stand" on these issues. For example, I needed to decide if I wanted the funeral ritual to be based on the premise that there was an afterlife after death or not. If at some later date, I want to take a different stand on these issues, I will simply adapt the funeral ritual to reflect my new spiritual beliefs.

Despite the difficulty involved in writing this chapter, in the end it gave me the most amount of satisfaction. The funerals I had participated in throughout my life had been such negative, alienating experiences that I felt a tremendous sense of relief to know that the next time someone I loved died, I would be prepared to arrange the kind of funeral I believed in.

I hope the following information will enable anyone dissatisfied with traditional funeral rituals to design alternatives that are suited to his/her needs and values. As I have stressed throughout, the alternative rituals that I present in this book are meant only as catalysts--examples from which people can draw ideas to design their own rituals.

This chapter contains the following:

1) Legal information regarding funerals

2) Pros and cons of various aspects of funerals to help you clarify what is best for you

3) Information on how to plan and facilitate the logistics of a funeral

4) Some sample funeral rituals

5) Information on how to pre-plan your own funeral

6) Some readings appropriate for alternative funerals

Before You Begin Planning an Alternative Funeral

The very first step you will need to take in order to either plan for an alternative funeral for a loved one, or to request one in your behalf, is to affirm your entitlement and power to do so. The funeral rituals in any culture tend to be viewed as sacred and inviolable. Therefore, you will encounter much social opposition when you go against the norm. For example, you are very likely to encounter disapproval, admonishment, and disgust from funeral directors when you challenge their idea of the "proper funeral." Even friends and relatives are likely to balk if you reject the accepted funeral practices because they are indoctrinated to accept, without question, what authority figures tell them funerals should be.

For example, if you bury your loved one in a cardboard box because you think the $1,000 for a "nice" casket would be better used in other ways, be ready for an onslaught of criticism. If you decide to conduct your own funeral/memorial service (for your deceased loved ones, that is) instead of having a clergy person facilitate, you may be considered blasphemous and indecent. You may also have difficulty with public agencies; you are likely to be disinformed or treated as if "you shouldn't be sticking your nose into places where it doesn't belong." You may even be given incorrect legal advice. You will have to be ready to be assertive to convince the given authority that what you are demanding is not illegal, just unusual. Many funeral procedures are customs not legal requirements, e.g., the practices of embalming or burial in a casket. Keep in mind that one of the reasons you will encounter so much resistance from authority figures when you reject the traditional funeral is that you are interfering with a cherished cultural value: profit. The funeral industry is big, big business is this country, and the people who are reaping huge profits from traditional funeral rituals are going to fight, tooth and nail, anyone who threatens their ability to continue earning a profit from funerals.

In the last twenty years, we have begun to see a movement for reform of funeral practices in this country. This reform was sparked by Jessica Mitford's revolutionary book, The American Way of Death, published in 1962. In this study, Ms. Mitford candidly exposes the corruption and deception that has characterized the U.S. funeral industry, and she also questions some of the absurdities of our funeral customs. The Consumers Union (The consumer advocacy agency headed by Ralph Nader) published another important book on the subject of funerals in 1977 entitled Funerals, Consumer's Last Rights, which has brought about further reform. Slowly but surely, there has been a significant change in public consciousness about funerals. Many people have expressed interest in exploring alternatives to the traditional funeral by forming Memorial Societies, which assist people in obtaining more personal, meaningful, and inexpensive funerals. Despite these reform movements, many families still bend under the social pressure to have traditional funerals.

One of the best ways to insure that you will be able to overcome the social pressures that might keep you from having the kind of funeral you believe in is to think about funeral arrangements ahead of time. Feel free to talk to your family about the type of funeral you would like, and encourage them to share their preferences with you. Many people feel uncomfortable thinking or talking about the details and logistics of their own funerals. Yet a funeral is held in your behalf, and it is therefore logical that you should have some input. Some information that made me feel more comfortable talking with my family about the kind of funeral I preferred be held in my behalf was reading about the funeral customs of the pioneers of the Appalachian area in a book entitled Foxfire 2. I learned it was a custom of pioneer Appalachian women to sew the dresses they wanted to be buried in themselves, and for men to make their own coffins. So pre-planning one's own funeral is not a new idea! More and more people are beginning to express their preferences regarding their funerals. Since people's religious/philosophical beliefs are becoming more and more varied, it is understandable that they have different ideas about the kind of funeral they might want, both in terms of body disposition and the service itself.

Familiarizing Yourself with the Laws Regarding Funerals

In order to plan an alternative funeral, it is necessary to become aware of the many laws that pertain to funerals. As you familiarize yourself with funeral laws and regulations, you will very quickly discover that your freedom in designing a funeral is extremely limited. However, it is better to become aware of the legal restrictions ahead of time. When people are unaware of funeral laws, they often unknowingly request funeral arrangements which are not legally possible. The surviving loved ones are often left feeling frustrated because they cannot carry out the express wishes of the deceased.

On the following pages is a list of laws that you need to be aware of either to make pre-arrangements for your own funeral or to plan for the funeral of a loved one.

Laws Which Will Affect Persons Making Pre-arrangements for Their Own Funerals

Laws Regarding Disposition of Body After Death

It may come as a complete surprise to you to learn that a person living in the United States does not have the right to determine how his/her body will be disposed of after death. Of course, there is the exception of donating one's body for research which will be discussed later in this chapter. As the laws currently stand, regardless of how detailed a will or "letter of instruction regarding my funeral arrangements" you may leave, your surviving kin are under no legal obligation to carry out your wishes. In fact, it quite often happens that the manner in which a person's body is dealt with after death directly violates his/her written directions. What may appear as the abuse of a right is merely the lack of specific legislation guaranteeing the right of a person to dictate how his/her body will be disposed of after death. Thus the Common Law prevails:

"Under the early English common law, no rights of property in a dead body were recognized. [22 Am Jur 2d Dead Bodies 4]. From

58

this it followed, quite logically, that a dead body could not be the subject of a testamentary bequest, and that a testator's directions for the disposal of his [her] remains were merely a request without probative effect.

American Law Review, 3rd Edition, Volume 7, pp. 748-9.

Though no one can own a dead body, there are laws as to who has the rights of possession of a dead body for the purposes of burial:

> "The courts have, however, created a right of possession (as opposed to the right of ownership) for purposes of disposition. A person's next of kin and executors have been held by the courts to have certain rights of possession over his body for the purpose of disposition which take precedence over the person's antemortem express and contrary wishes."

William A. Neilson and C. Gaylord Watkins, Proposals for Legislative Reform Aiding the Consumer of Funeral Industry Products and Services, Cello Press 1973, p. 14.

Who has the right to possession of a dead body? In accordance with legal guidelines, possession is determined in the following order of right:

1) Surviving spouse
2) Children of proper age
3) Parents
4) Brother or sister
5) Or more distant kin, as modified by any circumstances of special intimacy or association with the decedent.

Thus, as the law stands, a person has no absolute right to determine how his/her body will be dealt with after death. The right to decide is given to the kin, in the order specified above. An individual has no legal right to transfer that right from the specific kin to another person. For example, if you have lived with your lover unmarried for thirty years you cannot grant that person the right to determine your funeral arrangements.

Though there is no legislation that guarantees individuals the right to determine their own funeral arrangements, the matter can be taken to court. In cases where the next of kin plan to override the express wishes of the deceased, the matter can be taken to court by a friend or lover, or by other family members who are sympathetic to the wishes of the deceased. The court can overrule the common law. The common laws are very old, and judges are therefore sometimes willing to overlook them in light of existing circumstances. In such cases, the express wishes of the deceased are considered along with the opposing desires of other parties:

> "For the most part, it has been recognized that a decedent's expressed preference must be considered in the light of the surrounding circumstances and the wishes of interested parties, including the public, the religious or other institution...and the persons entitled to be heard by reason of association with or relationships to the

decedent, primarily his surviving spouse and next of kin."

Annotation entitled "Validity and Effect of Testamentary Direction as to the Disposition of Testator's Body", American Law Review, Volume 7, 3rd Edition, p. 747.

There are volumes and volumes of such cases, which you can read: controversies regarding funeral arrangements that are taken to court. Each case is decided on an individual basis. If you would like to see some examples of how the courts have ruled in various cases consult, (in addition to the one above), the following:

American Law Review, Volume 54, Third Edition, pp. 1037-1067: "Enforcement of Preference Expressed by Decedent as to Disposition Of His [Her] Body After Death."

In summary, there is no legislation which grants that an individual's stated wishes for funeral arrangements will be followed. The common law gives the next of kin the right to determine funeral arrangements making the decedent's wishes secondary. However, the matter can be taken to court, and sometimes the court will order the kin to respect the decedent's wishes. Therefore, if you plan to request an alternative funeral for yourself, it is very important that you detail your requests in writing. If there is controversy over these arrangements after your death, there is a chance that your wishes will still be upheld in court. If you make only verbal requests and there is a dispute, the chances are much slimmer that the courts will rule in favor of your wishes. How to put your preferences for funeral arrangements in writing is discussed later in this chapter.
There is one exception in which a person is guaranteed the right to determine how his/her body will be dealt with after death. "The Uniform Anatomical Gift Act" grants a person the right to donate his/her body for medical research without the legal interference of surviving kin. I believe that as of 1978 this act has been adopted by every state.

Excerpts from the U.S. Anatomical Gift Act

(Section 10102 03): "Any individual of sound mind and 18 years of age or more may give all or any physical part of the individual's body to:

a) Any hospital, surgeon, or physician for medical or dental education, research, advancement of medical or dental science, therapy, or transplantation.

b) Any accredited medical or dental school, college, or university for education, research, advancement of medical or dental science, or therapy.

c) Any bank or storage facility for medical or dental education, research, advancement of medical or dental science, therapy, or transplantation.

d) Any specified individual for therapy or transplantation by that individual.

e) Any approved or accredited school of optometry, nursing, or veterinary medicine.

...The rights of the donee [person or institution who receives gift of body or part thereof], created by the gift, are paramount to the rights of others...."

As the laws currently stand then, you can donate your body for research after death and this decision cannot be overridden by surviving kin. However, you have no guarantee about any other express requests for disposition of your body:

"And so we now have the irrational situation where, while one can donate one's body or parts of it and be reasonably certain that such instructions will be followed, the same certainty is not present for instructions about final disposition or the sort of funeral or memorial service, burial or cremation that one would like to have."

William A. Neilson and C. Gaylord Watkins, Proposals for Legislative Reform Aiding the Consumer of Funeral Products and Services, Cello Press, 1973, p. 15.

We are very much in need of legislation which guarantees, not just the right to donate one's body for research without veto, but a general right to dictate the means of final disposition of one's body and the type of funeral service given in one's behalf.

This need was addressed by Neilson and Watkins, two Canadian lawyers, in their book Proposals for Legislative Reform Aiding the Consumer of Funeral Industry Products and Services. In this booklet, Neilson and Watkins suggest that both the Canadian Model Tissue Act and the United States Uniform Anatomical Gift Act could be expanded upon to include a more general right of individuals to determine the method of disposition of their bodies after death, and the format/content of their funeral service. They outline what they think needs to be included in such legislation and why, and they draft a model legislative package, coined a Self-Disposition Act. They recommend that people send a copy to their legislators. I am re-printing with permission their legislative package.

I urge you to send a photocopy of this legislative package to your legislator. Change will only come about through political activism.

Self Disposition Act

A Legislative Package for Establishing the Right of Self Disposition

Preamble:

This Act enshrines and confers upon every individual the right to direct how his [her] body is to be disposed of after death and provides for the carrying out of these directions if made in a prescribed manner.

Citation/Short Title:

1. This Act may be cited as The Right of Self Disposition Act.

Definitions/ Interpretations:

2. Definitions of Frequently Used Terms:

(a) "Funeral Service Industry" encompasses the business of conducting funerals, including the sale of industry products and the furnishing of industry services and facilities incident to the care and preparation for burial and/or cremation or other final disposal of human remains.

(b) "Industry member" is any person, firm, corporation or organization engaged in the funeral service industry.

(c) "Industry products" are all articles and supplies, including, but not limited to, caskets, burial vaults, outside boxes, cremation urns, and other equipment used in the course of a funeral and of preparing human remains for burial and/or cremation or other final disposal thereof.

(d) "Industry services" refers to work done and acts performed by an industry member in the course of a funeral, including the care and preparation for burial and/or cremation or other final disposal of human remains.

(Source, proposed F.T.C. Trade Practice Rule, 1964)

(e) "Disposition" refers to the preparation for, type or place of disposal of human remains and includes all related acts, agreements, ceremonies, events and practices.

(f) "Writing" includes a will and any other testamentary instrument whether or not probate has been applied for and granted and whether or not the will or testamentary instrument is valid.

(Source: Canadian Model Human Tissue Act)

Right of Self Disposition and Manner of Exercising It:

CANADA

3. Any person who has attained the age of majority may direct:

    (a) in a writing signed by him [her] at any time

              or

    (b) orally in the presence of at least two witnesses during his [her] final illness; witnesses during his [her] final illness;

all aspects of the final disposition after death of his [her] remains.

(Source: Canadian Model Human Tissue Act)

UNITED STATES

3. (a) Any individual of sound mind and 18 years of age or older may direct the final disposition after death of his [her] body.

(b) The direction may be made by will and shall become effective upon the death of the testator without waiting for probate. If will is not probated or if it is declared invalid for testamentary purposes, the direction, to the extent it has been acted upon in good faith, shall nevertheless be valid and effective.

(c) The direction may also be made by document other than a will and shall become effective on the death of the person giving the directions. The document shall be signed by the person giving the direction in the presence of two witnesses, who shall sign the document in his [her] presence. If the person giving the direction cannot sign, then the document may be signed for him [her] as he [she] directs and in the presence of two witnesses who shall sign the document in his [her] presence.

(Source: Uniform Anatomical Gift Act)

Minors/under 18:

CANADA/UNITED STATES

4. Notwithstanding section 3, a direction given by a person who has not attained the age of majority/18 is valid for the purposes of this Act

if the persons who acted upon it had no reason to believe that the person who gave it had not attained the age of majority/18.

(Source: Canadian Model Human Tissue Act)

Responsibility For Disposition:

5. Responsibility for disposition of a person's body after death rests upon the following persons in the order named:

   a) the surviving spouse;
   b) the surviving children;
   c) the surviving parents;
   d) the next of kin;
   e) the personal representatives of the deceased;
   f) persons making use of the body or parts thereof pursuant to parts thereof pursuant to the Model Act/Uniform Act;
   g) the local governmental authority in the locality concerned in the manner provided by law.

Persons Bound By Directions:

6. The directions of the deceased for disposition made in accordance with subsection 4(1) are to the extent financially possible binding upon and paramount to the contrary wishes of all persons who are responsible for or become involved in the disposition of a person's body after death including:

   (a) persons providing or supplying funeral services related to the disposition; and

   (b) persons named as responsible in subsection (1) above but for persons making use of the body or parts thereof pursuant to the Model Human Tissue Act, the deceased's directions for disposition are binding only to the extent that the use is not frustrated.

Duty To Determine if Directions Made:

7. Persons upon whom the deceased's directions for disposition are binding, if made, shall determine with diligence appropriate to the circumstances whether the deceased did in fact make directions for disposition that comply with subsection 4(1).

If No Directions: Limitations on Disbursement:

8. If no directions have been made or if no directions can be found, disposition shall be arranged by the person or persons responsible in a way that will not excessively deplete the deceased's estate or other available funds.

Conflict:

9. In the event of conflict between different directions for

disposition by the deceased, the most recent direction complying with this Act shall prevail provided that implementing the direction will not frustrate use of the body or parts thereof pursuant to consent given or gift made that conforms with the Model Human Tissue/Uniform Anatomical Gift Act.

Mandatory Record-Keeping:

10. All persons using bodies or parts thereof pursuant to the Model Human Tissue/Uniform Anatomical Gift Act and all funeral service industry members who provide or supply industry products or services shall keep on file for all dispositions in which they become involved copies of the deceased's directions for disposition, if available, and a record indicating the manner of final disposition.

Availability Of Records:

11. This information shall be made available on reasonable notice to:

(a) persons bearing responsibility for disposition;

(b) the personal representatives of the deceased;

(c) government officials or regulatory authorities charged with enforcing this legislation or with governance of the funeral service industry.

Offence:

12. Every person who knowingly or negligently contravenes any provision of this Act, or more particularly, ignores directions for dispositions valid under this Act is guilty of an offense and on summary conviction is liable to a fine of not more than $1,000 dollars or to imprisonment for a term of not more than six months, or to both.

Prima Facie Offence:

13. Any discrepancies between a deceased's direction for disposition and an industry member's records indicating the manner of final disposition shall be treated, as prima facie evidence of an offense under this Act.

Laws Affecting Funerals in General

Since funerals practices are, for the most part, regulated by the states, not the federal government, putting together a list of all the laws affecting funerals would be a time consuming and tedious endeavor. Such a task was beyond the scope of this book. However, I thought it would be helpful to list the aspects of funerals that are likely to be regulated by state law. To determine which of the aspects of funerals listed below are regulated by your state, and how, write to your state licensing and regulation board. They will send you information on funeral regulations free of charge.

1) Moving a Dead Body: In some states, only a funeral director can move a dead body. This means that even if you are planning a direct burial or cremation, you cannot transport the body to the cemetery or crematorium yourself. Crematoriums and cemeteries will not accept a body without a burial transit permit, and in some states only a funeral director can obtain this permit. Check with your state licensing board.

Author's Note:
In states which do not require a funeral director, people are taking the body of their deceased loved ones to cemeteries or crematoriums themselves and saving several hundred dollars by doing so. In researching this chapter, I read various articles by people who had chosen to deal with their deceased loved one's body themselves instead of having a funeral director do it for them. They described the experience as being extremely therapeutic, stressing how empowering and comforting it felt to care for the body of their loved one instead of delegating this very personal task to a complete stranger.

2) Where Bodies Can Be Laid Out: In some states (Michigan, for one), law permits persons to have the body of a loved one laid out in their own homes instead of at a funeral home if they so desire. Of course, the law may or may not require that a funeral director transport the body to and from the home.

3) Embalming: Embalming is not automatically required in any state. The circumstances under which embalming is required vary greatly from state to state. Some states do not require embalming under any circumstances. Some states require embalming if there is to be viewing of the body during the funeral service. Some other instances in which states require embalming are: when there is to be a period of wait between death and disposition of the body (the waiting period allowed varies); when the body is to be transported by common carrier; and when the deceased died of a serious communicable disease.

To determine the specific regulations in effect in your state consult your state licensing board or Funerals, Consumers' Last Rights published by The Consumers' Union. This book contains a complete list of legal embalming requirements in each state.

There are many documented examples of funeral directors telling people that embalming is required when it isn't, so make sure that you are not disinformed. In 1975 the Federal Trade Commission (F.T.C.) enacted a ruling which states that funeral directors must inform customers that embalming is not required except in certain limited circumstances. This F.T.C. ruling also prohibits funeral directors from embalming bodies without prior permission from kin.

Author's Note:

If you are unfamilar with what exactly the process of embalming involves, there is an excellent description of embalming in the book Funerals: Consumers' Last Rights, by The Consumers' Union.

4) Caskets: Though state law may require that a body be enclosed in a casket for cremation or burial, the definition of what constitutes a casket may be interpreted in many ways. In many states a cloth bag or cardboard box can qualify as a casket. So if you do not want to be buried in a traditional casket, find out if caskets are required in your state and, if so, what specifically the state law defines as a casket.

Author's Note:

If you do want to use a casket, but do not want an expensive one, do not feel inhibited to ask the funeral director about plain pine boxes. Funeral directors usually have only expensive, ornate caskets on display, but simple wood ones are available.

5) Burial Vaults: A burial vault is a box, usually made of steel or cement that coffins are enclosed in before burial. Whether or not burial vaults are required varies from state to state. However, in many states it is the cemeteries, not state laws, that require vaults. Cemeteries that insist on vaults do so purely for profit. If a casket is buried without a vault, within a year or two, the grave will fall approximately one foot as the casket and body decay. The cemetery then has to fill in the grave and re-sod. Thus, to avoid the cost of refilling and re-sodding graves, cemeteries require vaults. The cost of a vault can range anywhere from $300 for a simple cement one, up to thousands of dollars for fancy steel ones.

If you desire to not use a burial vault, find out whether they are required by law in your state. If not, you may be able to find a cemetery that does not require them. Check out small rural cemeteries or ones that are publicly or cooperatively owned. Unfortunately, if all the cemeteries in your area require burial vaults, you may be required to use one.

Funeral directors and vault companies will of course tell you how wonderfully a vault will preserve the body of your loved one (preserve it for what, you might ask), but even the F.T.C. has determined that this claim is questionable.

6) Cremation: If you lived in a Third World country like India, you could build a funeral pyre of pine branches, cremate your loved one, and cast the ashes to the winds. However, in the United States the entire cremation process is highly regulated from beginning to end. First, you cannot, in any state, cremate your loved one yourself. Instead you have to hire a professional, profit-making person to cremate your loved one for you in a $1,000,000 crematorium, and pay anywhere from $250 to $1,000 for this service. Second, many states prohibit anyone but clergymembers, funeral directors, and crematorium personnel to be present in the cremation room; family are completely removed from the process. When family return after a specified time (usually from eight to twelve hours), they are simply handed a "shoe box" full of crushed ashes to dispose of. But, you have to be careful

where you scatter those ashes--there may be a law against it! Many states have rules about where ashes can and cannot be scattered.

I suspect that most people pay little heed to laws about scattering ashes. However, if you think that it might be illegal to scatter ashes where you intend to, e.g., in a national park, or waterway, you should avoid making public announcement of your intention. Don't state, in the obituary, for example, that the ashes will be scattered at such and such National Park.

Additional Note:

When deciding on a place to scatter ashes, make sure you take into account how the area may change in the future. If, for instance, you scatter your brother's ashes in the back yard under the willow tree, or in a wooded area he walked in every week, you may be disheartened if in a few years, the area is re-zoned and subsequently turned into a strip of McDonald's, Seven-Eleven stores and gas stations, or the city dump. That is one positive aspect of cemeteries: they are sacred ground; you can be assured that if, in the future, you want to go to the place where your loved one's physical remains were interred, you will have peace and solitude. Thus, if you scatter ashes, it is probably better to do so in a state or national park, or a river or lake, all of which are protected from the ravages of urban development.

Laws Regarding Actual Funeral/Memorial Service

There is no specific legislation in the United States which grants an individual the right to determine the content/format of his/her funeral/memorial service. That is, a person does not have the legal right to appoint someone to be in charge of arranging his/her funeral/memorial service. That right automatically, by common law, goes to family members in a prescribed order--the same order as for disposition of the body: surviving spouse, adult children, parents, siblings. When there is controversy between what the deceased requested regarding funeral service arrangements and what the surviving kin desires, the matter will be decided on a case by case basis in court. (The matter could be brought to court by surviving kin or a friend of the deceased who was sympathetic to the wishes of the deceased.) The courts may uphold the wishes of the deceased over contrary wishes by surviving kin, or vice-versa. As is the case with preferences for body disposition, it is very important that you detail, in writing, your preferences regarding funeral content and format. This will greatly increase the likelihood that your wishes will be followed.

The right to dictate the nature of one's funeral service, could, like a general right to determine the method of disposition of one's body after death, be guaranteed by a legislative act. But at this time no such law exists. However, it would be possible to amend The U.S. Anatomical Gift Act to both guarantee individuals the right to determine the method of disposition of their body after death and the right to determine the content and format of any funeral/memorial services held in their honor. I personally think that the right to determine the kind of funeral/memorial service one is given is just as important as being able to determine how one's body is dealt with after death. The legislative package drafted by Neilson and Watkins just discussed includes the right of an individual to determine the nature of his/her funeral service, as well as to decide the method of body disposition (See section 2e). Again, I urge you to send a copy of this legislative package to your legislators.

Deciding on Method of Body Disposition After Death

After reading up to this point you are now familiar with the laws that will affect you in pre-arranging your own funeral or in planning for the funeral of a loved one. The next step is to clarify what your preferences are in regard to body disposition and funeral services, within the options legally available to you.

Since our society has a kind of taboo against something so "distasteful" as discussing funeral arrangements, most people have little opportunity to discuss their preferences. I therefore thought it would be useful to readers to include the following list of pros and cons regarding the various methods of body disposition: burial, cremation, and donation of body for scientific research. I derived this list from approximately two hundred interviews. In the interviews, I asked people how they wanted their body dealt with after their death, and the reasons for their preferences.

Since most people are quite unfamiliar with the logistics of body disposition, I found that the interviewees' answers regarding body disposition were sometimes based on misinformation. I have therefore included "Author's Notes" to inform the reader of the inaccuracies unintentionally put forth by the interviewees.

Pros and Cons of Various Options for Body Disposition

BURIAL

Pros

1) Many people feel burial is the most "natural" method. Returning bodies to the earth for simple decomposition is the way Nature deals with the deaths of plants and animals.

Author's Note:

Unfortunately, many cemeteries have restrictions that require burial vaults. This obviously greatly detracts from the feeling of naturalness in returning ones body to the earth for decomposition. Vaults are made of materials like cement, steel, aluminum, and fiberglass, none of which are very conducive to decomposition. If it is important to you to be able to be buried without a vault, be sure you find out ahead of time if the cemeteries in your area require vaults for burial. If all cemeteries in your area do require vaults, research cemeteries that are in a more rural part of your state. They may be less likely to require them.

2) Having a burial site gives surviving family and friends a physical place to go to when they want to communicate with the deceased person. Many people find visiting the grave an excellent way to resolve feelings of grief. Many people report having very significant conversations at the grave-site of a loved one.

3) Burial is something that family and friends can do themselves. You can be with the body the entire time. Some cemeteries will allow family to help fill in the grave. With cremation, you have to turn the body over to a stranger and cannot even be present for the cremation. You are simply handed a box of ashes; you are completely removed from the process.

Cons

1) Many people feel that graves are depressing. They do not feel the need to be connected with a person's physical remains, since they feel that the body has no significance once the spirit has left it. Some people do not find going to a grave a useful way to communicate with the deceased. They would rather scatter the ashes on a mountain top or in the sea, and sit on the mountain top or walk along the seashore when they want to think of the deceased.

2) Some people find the atmosphere of cemeteries ostentatious. They are turned off by what they view as competition between survivors to see who can buy the largest tombstone.

3) A significant number of people stated that they would prefer burial if cemeteries were radically different.   They liked the idea of burial, but they didn't like that so much land had to be set aside for the sole purpose of cemeteries. They stated that they would like to be buried on land that was used for community gardens, parks, or playgrounds. In this hypothetical situation, everyone buried in the cemetery would know ahead of time that as soon as the cemetery was filled, it would be turned into a park.

Author's Note:

Due to space problems caused by the population explosion, this is an idea likely to be explored in the future. In fact, the government is considering turning closed cemeteries into parks. (A closed cemetery is one in which the last person was buried at least 120 years ago.) However, I think it would be better to convert a cemetery into a park or garden as soon as it was full. Instead of having grave stones, which compartmentalize the land making it almost impossible to walk around on and enjoy, I would envision one monument on which everyone's name who was buried there would be engraved.

DONATION OF BODY FOR RESEARCH/TRANSPLANTATION

Pros

This idea was preferred by a significant number of people because they liked the idea that by donating their body, they could extend the life of another human being, give sight to the blind, hearing to the deaf, etc. People also felt that by donating their body for research they would enable medical researchers to gain valuable information which would enhance the physical health of people for years to come. The idea of one's body being used for "something useful" or "my death helping the living" instead of "wasting space in a cemetery" or becoming "useless ashes" are sentiments expressed by proponents of this method of body disposition.

2) Saving the costs of funerals was another reason given for this preference. Donating one's body for research has significant financial benefits because most of the time there is no cost at all. The medical school or other institution will pick up the body, fill out necessary papers, and cremate and inter the physical remains after they have been used for research. The exact amount to be saved by donating one's body is of course difficult to determine. The least expensive, simple, direct, cremation ranges from $300 to $600. The least expensive, simple direct burial ranges anywhere from $800 to $1,600. These prices fluctuate greatly

depending on state, city, and other specifics. Thus, the savings can range anywhere from $300 to $1,600. Of course, the savings could be as much as $4,000 if the family was going to spend that much on the funeral.

Cons

1) There are a significant number of people who have disagreements with many of the practices and values of American medical practitioners. Many people feel that they are misinformed, financially ripped off, used as guinea pigs, and treated with disrespect by doctors. They are thus reluctant to donate their body to aid a profession whose integrity they question. Some people also feel that much of the time, energy, and money consumed in medical research would be better used in other ways. I.e., does it make sense to spend $100,000/per year or more for advanced medical technology to keep one ailing, over-sixty American alive, (whose disease was more than likely caused by over-consumption of alcohol, tobacco, and high fat diet) because he/she is rich enough to pay for it? Some question whether this money could be better used to feed starving Third World children. Some people don't like the idea of donating their bodies for medical research because they do not want to contribute to a health-care system which they see as elitist, corrupt, and misguided in its values.

2) Some people worry that their bodies will not be treated with respect and/or disposed of properly.

Author's Note:
Though there may have been neglect and abuse years ago, I am convinced by a report by The Consumers' Union, that these fears are ungrounded at this time. Current day practices are regulated, and as a result, medical schools, etc. are very careful to treat bodies with respect. Institutions using bodies for research also have their own crematoriums now, and when they are done using the bodies, they cremate the remains. The ashes are then buried. Often medical schools even have a chaplain perform a service for the remains during which they thank the people for their gift of their body for service to humanity.

3) Some people find the idea of people cutting up their bodies repulsive.

Author's Note:
Though we are certainly all entitled to our preferences, I have to say that I find this reasoning somewhat comical. If I were to worry about what happened to my body after death, I don't find the idea of worms crawling in and out of my body, or my body being burned, any less repulsive than having it cut up.

CREMATION

Pros

1) Like donating one's body for research, financial savings was one of the reasons stated for preferring cremation. It is difficult to estimate the exact difference in costs, as there are so many variables. The price of the least expensive, simple, direct cremation ranges from $300 to $600., and the price of the least expensive, simple, direct burial ranges from $800 to $1600. The average price difference ranges from $500 to $1,000.

2) Among respondents who favored cremation, most preferred it as an option because of the freedom to have one's ashes scattered wherever one chooses. Many people like the idea of their ashes being scattered at sea, on a mountain top, or in a river so that their surviving family and friends can go to a beautiful natural place to think of them rather than to "a compartmentalized grave site in a dreary cemetery."

3) Cremation is particularly popular among people who think that there is no significance to their physical remains after death. These people like the idea of their remains being transformed into the simplest elemental form and cast to the wind or sea with no further thought given to them. They don't like the idea of there being a grave site for their physical remains that has to be perpetually mowed and cared for, all for the "silly purpose" of housing their physical remains.

Cons

1) The process of cremation is more impersonal and non-participatory. With burial the surviving family and friends can be present during the lowering of the body into the grave, and can help close the grave; family members are not legally allowed to be present during cremation. They are simply handed a box of ashes.

2) Cremation is disliked by some people because it is "high tech." A significant amount of natural gas is used in the cremation process because it is done at such high temperatures. "Why use precious fossil fuels to decompose a body when Mother Nature will do it for free?" These people also think the $1,000,000 cost of the crematorium itself is a wasteful expenditure.

ANOTHER ISSUE TO DECIDE--OPEN VS. CLOSED CASKET

Another preference you should address in pre-planning your funeral is whether you would like surviving family and friends to have the opportunity to view your body after your death. Below is a list of pro and con statements regarding open vs. closed caskets compiled from the above mentioned interviews.

Pros

1) "Looking at the body of the deceased person helps me to deal with the idea that he/she is dead. Once I was not informed of the death of a friend who lived out of state, and I therefore did not attend his funeral. For years it was difficult for me to really grasp that he was dead. Though I disagree with the usual ostentatious display of fancy casket and expensive flowers, I do think viewing the body is therapeutic."

Cons

1) "I think looking at people after they are dead is gross and disgusting. I keep flashing back to how my grandfather looked in his casket instead of remembering how he looked alive."

2) "I don't want to have an open casket because I don't want to be embalmed. I don't want anyone touching my body for three days after death because it takes three days for the spirit to leave the physical body. Embalming interferes with the spirit leaving the body. Besides I don't want anybody injecting chemicals into my body, even after I'm dead."

Author's Note:

If you wanted to have an open casket for three days, you would have to be embalmed in some states but not all. However, in most states, you could have an open casket, without having to be embalmed, for 24 to 48 hours. Having an open casket, therefore, does not necessarily mean that you would have to be embalmed.

In summary, I hope the ideas discussed above will help you clarify what your own personal preferences are regarding body disposition. There are definitely pros and cons to each option and each person has to decide what feels best for himself/herself. Last, I would like to include a recent personal experience I had in deciding among various methods of body disposition. It was, for me, a firsthand experience of the pros and cons of various methods of body disposition.

During the process of writing this chapter, I had the sad and ironic experience of my dog dying unexpectedly. As I struggled with my partner to choose among various methods of body disposition, I felt angry and sad; none of the options felt very good. Should we sneak into a state park and bury my dog so her remains could be in a natural, beautiful place as I would like? Yet what if we were caught doing it, or if her grave is later dug up because a park ranger thinks a dead human body has been concealed there? Should we get her body cremated? The cremation process seemed so unnatural and high-tech, particularly for a dog. Yet at least then I could scatter her ashes in a park without fear of being caught. Should I bury her in my backyard? No, because I live a mobile lifestyle and her grave would soon be in someone else's back yard, which wouldn't feel right. And the pet cemetery, a flat field of compartmentalized graves, didn't seem like anywhere I could ever visit; nor did it seem like a fitting place for the remains of my free-spirited dog.

My partner and I finally decided on cremation as the best of several lousy options. We drove her to the crematory ourselves. However, I had a difficult time surrendering my dog's body to the cold, "high-tech," impersonal-looking machine. My aversion heightened as the crematory attendant impersonally hoisted my dog's body, and unceremoniously dumped her into the retort oven.

Upon being handed, several hours later, the burned remains of my dog's body in a plastic container, I felt a sinking, nauseous feeling in my stomach. The ashes were so useless looking. If I had buried her, she could have helped fertilize the earth.

Scattering my dog's ashes in the river where we had swum together was a comforting and therapeutic experience. We said prayers for her spirit to flow on as the river.

I lay at home that night crying and emotionally spent. I realized that the whole experience of death had been made all the more painful because of all the restrictions society inflicted upon me. I struggled for some thought to make my frustration easier to bear. Sad as I was, it came to me. Why expect a society that treats people and animals with such disregard, in life, to treat them any better in death? However, I do not want to end this chapter on such a negative note, so let me add the following: Despite the insane and self-destructive state of our society, we are, I believe, in our roundabout, stumbling ways, evolving toward a more healthy and harmonious state of being. As our society evolves towards a greater state of health, we can be assured that our death customs will likewise become more positive, therapeutic experiences.

Deciding on the Type of Funeral/Memorial Service

I have heard a significant number of people state that they do not want <u>any</u> funeral/memorial service held in their honor after their death. Many people are so alienated by the ostentatiousness, elitism, and archaic religious aspects of the traditional funeral that they are completely turned off to the idea of funeral services in general. Many other people are arranging traditional funeral services for their deceased loved ones but feeling dismayed that the services are incongruent with their philosophical beliefs. If you are someone who is dissatisfied with the traditional funeral rituals of our culture I hope you will find the following information on alternative funeral services helpful.

I became interested in designing an alternative funeral service because the funeral services I had attended over the past fifteen years left me feeling extremely alienated and dissatisfied. I found the traditional funeral's ostentatious display of an elaborate casket and baskets upon baskets of outrageously priced flowers repugnant. In addition, I found myself very dissatisfied with traditional funeral services because of their Christian orientation. The Christian concept of life after death was very much in conflict with my own beliefs. I no longer believed that after death I was going to Heaven to play harps with God the Father. I no longer believed in the concept of Heaven, nor in God as a paternal personality.* I therefore found Christian funeral services far from soothing and comforting.

I also felt dissatisfied with Christian funeral services because of their hierarchical nature. I was uncomfortable with the idea of a clergy person being called in as "the expert" to facilitate a funeral service. It made much more sense to me for a member of the family or a friend of the deceased, by virtue of close association to the deceased, to be the facilitator rather than a stranger. The funeral service would thus be free of any hierarchical power structure. It would simply be an egalitarian coming together of people who had known and loved the deceased person, to share their grief and to help one another cope with the pain surrounding death.

Being thus dissatisfied with traditional funeral services I decided to write a funeral service which reflected my spiritual orientation. I hope that by presenting some alternatives to the traditional funeral I can introduce people to some ideas for funeral services that might be more congruent with their needs and values. It is my intention that the services I have written will serve as inspiration for people to design their own funeral services unique to their needs.

---

* See Chapter 1 for a detailed account of my disagreements with Christianity.

Introduction to an Alternative Funeral Service

I felt an initial sense of uncertainty when I set about trying to write this funeral service. I, like most people in our culture, was used to having clergy facilitate my rituals for me. However, I was so dissatisfied with Christian funerals that I was determined to develop some alternative funeral rituals, despite my misgivings.

I began with a brainstorming session. I wrote down whatever ideas came to mind--what might make sense to include in a funeral/memorial service. I quickly discovered, however, that designing a funeral service was a complex endeavor. In order to write a funeral service, it was necessary that I clarify my thoughts about number of religious/philosophical issues. Inherent in a funeral ritual are certain assumptions about God, after-life, the meaning of life, etc., and I had to decide what perspective I wanted my funeral ritual to reflect on these issues. I knew I didn't like Christianity's explanation of these issues, but, on the other hand, I didn't know what I believed with respect to questions like whether there was life after death.

After doing a tremendous amount of soul searching, as well as a lot of reading, I resolved my thoughts and feelings about these philosophical issues enough to write the funeral ritual. I realized I could go on indefinitely contemplating questions like the meaning of life and death. However, if I ever wanted to finish my funeral ritual, I needed to simply take a stand on these issues. If later my views on life after death changed, I could design a new ritual. I decided, therefore, to write a funeral ritual which reflected the perspective that there was life after death. However, since I had spent many years of my life as an atheist, I also decided to write a funeral ritual with an atheist orientation. This chapter thus contains two funeral rituals; this one which reflects a belief in life after death and one which has an atheist orientation.

An important part of my designing these alternative funeral services, besides my own introspections, was soliciting feedback and ideas from friends. After I wrote my rough drafts of the funeral services, I handed the drafts out to approximately thirty people, with extensive questionnaires. I was amazed at how enthusiastically people responded to the opportunity to give their opinions about funerals. I used the feedback I received to improve the funeral services, and slowly but surely, I developed some workable alternative funeral services.

Although I found it impossible, as I just mentioned, to write these rituals without putting some of my own personal religious values into them, I have tried to write them in such a way as to be applicable for other people. In addition to two sample funeral services, I have included a general outline for designing/facilitating an alternative funeral service, which I hope can assist people in designing their own funeral services. I have also included as part of this chapter, a collection of inspirational readings suitable for funerals. I collected these reading from a variety of books, and also received suggested readings from friends. Thus, a person can tailor these funeral rituals to his/her particular needs by inserting readings that reflect his/her beliefs.

An Alternative Funeral Service

Facilitator:

We have all come together today to share our sadness over the death of someone we all love very dearly. We also come together to renew our faith that death has a divine purpose, and to communicate our love, appreciation, and hopes to _____ as he/she begins a new part of his/her spiritual journey.

(Pause)

Facilitator:

We know death is but a passage to another existence filled with more joy and challenges. Yet we feel a grief and sadness at this parting. We feel a pain that reaches into the depth of our being. There are no words that can take away our sadness; it is something we must live with. For our sadness comes out of our ability to love, and it is love that gives richness and joy to our lives. It is our love for _____ that is causing our sadness. Yet, as much as we would like to wish away this sadness, we would not want to wish away our ability to love. Let us seek comfort in our sadness in the words of the poet Gibran. Let us read together:

Facilitator and Guests:
(In Unison)

> *When love beckons to you, follow him,**
> *Though his ways are hard and steep,*
> *And when his wings enfold you yield to him,*
> *Though the sword hidden among his pinions may wound you.*
> *And when he speaks to you believe in him,*
> *Though his voice may shatter your dreams as the north wind lays waste the garden.*
>
> *For even as love crowns you so shall he crucify you. Even as he is for your growth so is he for your pruning.*
> *Even as he ascends to your height and caresses your tenderest branches that quiver in the sun,*
> *So shall he descend to your roots and shake them in their clinging to the earth.*
>
> *...If in your fear you would seek only love's peace and love's pleasure,*
> *Then it is better for you that you cover*

76

your nakedness and pass out of love's
threshing-floor.

Into the seasonless world where you
shall laugh, but not all of your laughter,
and weep, but not all of your tears.

Reprinted from <u>*THE PROPHET*</u>*, by*
Kahlil Gibran, by permission of Alfred A.
Knopf, Inc. Copyright 1923 by Kahlil
Gibran and renewed 1951 by administrators
C.T.A. of the Kahlil Gibran estate and Mary
G. Gibran. pp. 11, 12.

* *Author's Note:*

    I would prefer that this poem did not
contain male pronouns which I consider sexist.
However, I think Gibran's poetry is unmatched
in beauty and wisdom. It was written in the
1920's before people were conscious of sexist
language. When I use this poem in my own
rituals, I rewrite it, removing the sexist
pronouns. However, for publication, I must
reprint an author's work as originally written.

Facilitator:
    As we weep and grieve, let us also rejoice that we have known the joys of love. Let us also remember that we would not trade away that joy even to escape this sadness.

(Pause)

Facilitator:
    Though death brings sadness, we must remember that death also brings re-birth. Let us renew our faith that death has a divine purpose by listening to the words of Edward Carpenter.

Reader:

Among the Ferns

I lay among the ferns,
Where they lifted their fronds, innumerable, in the greenwood
   wilderness, like wings winnowing the air;
And their voices went by me continually.

And I listened, and Lo! softly inaudibly raining I heard not
   the voices of the ferns only, but of all living creatures:
Voices of mountain and star,
Of cloud and forest and ocean,

And of little rills tumbling among the rocks,
And of the high tops where the moss-beds are and the springs
arise.
As the wind at midday rains whitening over the grass,
As the night-bird glimmers a moment, fleeting between the
lonely watcher and the moon,
So softly inaudibly they rained,
While I sat silent.

And in the silence of the greenwood I knew the secret of the
growth of the ferns;
I saw their delicate leaflets tremble breathing an undescribed
and unuttered life;
And, below, the ocean lay sleeping;
And round them the mountains and the stars dawned in glad
companionship forever.

And a voice came to me, saying:
In every creature, in forest and ocean, in leaf and tree and bird
and beast and man, there moves spirit other than
its mortal own
Pure, fluid, as air--intense as fire,
Which looks abroad and passes along the spirits of all other
creatures, drawing them close to itself,
Nor dreams of other law than that of perfect equality;
And this is the spirit of immortality and peace.

And whatsoever creature hath this spirit, to it
No harm can befall, for wherever it goes it has its nested home
and to it every loss comes charged with an equal gain;
It gives--but to receive a thousand-fold;
It yields its life--but at the hands of love;
And death is the law of its eternal growth.

And I saw that was the law of every creature--that this spirit
should enter in and take possession of it,
That it might have no more fear nor doubt or be at war within
itself any longer.
And, lo! in the greenwood all around me it moved,
Where the sunlight floated fragrant under the boughs,
And the fern-fronds winnowed the air;
In the oak-leaves dead of last year, and the small shy things
that rustled among them;
In the songs of the birds, and the broad shadowing leaves
overhead;
In the fields sleeping below, and in the river and the high
dreaming air;
Gleaming ecstatic it moved--with joy incarnate.
And it seemd to me, as I looked, that it penetrated these things
suffusing them;
And wherever it penetrated, behold there was nothing left
down to the smallest atom which was not winged spirit

instinct with life.

Who shall understand the words of the ferns lifting their
    fronds unnumerable?
What man shall go forth into the world, holding his life
    in his open palm--
With high adventurous joy from sunrise to sunset--
Fearless, in his sleeve laughing, having outflanked his enemies?
His heart like nature's garden--that all men abide in--
Free, where the great winds blow, rains fall, and the sun shines,
And manifold growths come forth and scatter their fragrance?
Who shall be like a grave, where men may bury
Sin and sorrow and shame, to rise in the new day
Glorious out of their grave? who, deeply listening,
Shall hear through all his soul the voices of all creation,
Voices of mountain and star, voices of old men
Softly audibly raining? shall seize and fix them,
Rivet them fast with love, no more to lose them?
Who shall be that spirit of deep fulfillment,
Himself, self-centered? Yet evermore from that centre
Over the world expanding, along all creatures
Loyally passing--with love, with perfect equality?

Him immortality crowns. In him all sorrow
And mortal passion of death shall pass from creation.
They who sit by the road and are weary shall rise up
As he passes. Those who despair shall arise.
Who shall understand the words of the ferns winnowing the
    air?
 Death shall change as the light in the morning changes:
 Death shall change as the light 'twixt moonset and dawn.

Edward Carpenter, Towards Democracy, London, George
Allen & Unwin L.T.D., 1949, pp. 151--154.

Author's Note:
I again apologize for the sexism. I had difficulty finding
appropriate poems for funerals, and was therefore reluctant
to omit good poems because of their sexist pronouns. As I
mentioned before, when I use poems in my rituals, I rewrite
them removing the sexist pronouns.

Facilitator starts music.

Facilitator:
    Though _____ is no longer with us, he/she will live on through the many gifts he/she has given us during her/his lifetime. Let us take time today to share with one another the gifts that _____ has given each of us during his/her lifetime. Please form a circle. Let us share with each other how _____ contributed to our growth and happiness during his/her lifetime.

79

(Allow ample time for each person to speak for a few minutes. Crying should not be discouraged; it is part of the grieving process.)

Facilitator:

In order to help _____ in his/her passage from this lifetime to the next stage in his/her existence, let us express our gratitude to _____ for all the gifts he/she has given us in his/her lifetime. Let us join hands and join together in sending a silent prayer of thanks, love, and encouragement to _____ in his/her new realm of existence.

(Pause)

Facilitator:

As we are faced with death again, we are reminded that our lives on this plane will end too. In order to be able to face our own deaths with calmness and serenity, we need to take this opportunity to reaffirm our commitment to use our lives to the best of our abilities, to further the growth and evolution of our spirits. May _____'s death be a catalyst for each of us to reattune ourselves to our unique goals and purposes in this lifetime. May we leave here today with a renewed commitment to use each day of our lives to manifest our potential as fully as possible.

Facilitator:

Let us remember, in the coming months, to take time in our lives to continue our grieving process, which today has just begun. In order to heal our grief, let us remember to not block but fully experience <u>all</u> of our feelings. In closing, let us remember to share our sadness with one another--for in sharing our grief, each of our burdens are made lighter.

Facilitator:

_____'s daughter _____ will scatter his ashes in Rocky Mountain National Park as he requested.

Facilitator:

The family wishes to thank everyone for attending. The service is ended. Go in peace.

An Atheist Funeral Service

INTRODUCTION

It was a real challenge for me to try and write an atheist funeral service. I come from a family in which some members are atheists, and for many years I considered myself one. I think death is much more painful for atheists because they cannot console themselves with the idea that the deceased is going on to heaven or another life. I think back to the times when I didn't believe in an after-life and remember how painful funeral services were for me. I found none of the words consoling, because I didn't believe any of the comforting ideas about an after-life to be true. Since the service was of no help to me, I was left to struggle and grapple with a way to understand and cope with death myself. Though I am no longer an atheist, the memory of that pain and confusion led me to write the following service. I hope that it will help people who do not believe in God or an after-life find comfort at the time of death of a loved one.

An Atheist Funeral Service

Facilitator:

We have all come together today to share our sadness over the death of someone we all love very dearly. We feel a grief today that reaches into the depth of our being. There are no words that can take away our sadness; it is something we must live with. Yet this painful sadness is born out of the joy we have felt in knowing and loving _____. As much as we would like to wish away this sadness, we would not want to wish away the joy we have experienced from having _____ as a part of our lives. Let us seek comfort in our sadness in the words of the poet Gibran. Let us read together:

Facilitator and Guests:
   (In Unison)

> *Your joy is your sorrow unmasked.*
> *And the selfsame well from which your*
> *laughter rises was oftentimes filled with your*
> *tears.*
> *And how else can it be?*
> *The deeper that sorrow carves into your*
> *being, the more joy you can contain.*
> *Is not the cup that holds your wine the very*
> *cup that was burned in the potter's oven?*
> *And is not the lute that soothes your*
> *spirit, the very wood that was hollowed*
> *with knives?*
> *When you are joyous, look deep into*
> *your heart and you shall find it is only that*
> *which has given you sorrow that is giving*
> *you joy.*
> *When you are sorrowful look again in*
> *your heart, and you shall see that in truth*
> *you are weeping for that which has been*
> *your delight.*
> *Some of you say, "Joy is greater than*
> *sorrow," and others say, "Nay sorrow is*
> *the greater."*
> *But I say unto you, they are inseparable.*

Reprinted from THE PROPHET, *by Kahlil Gibran, by permission of Alfred A. Knopf, Inc. Copyright 1923 by Kahlil Gibran and renewed 1951 by administrators C.T.A. of the Kahlil Gibran estate and Mary G. Gibran, pp. 29, 30.*

Facilitator:

As we weep and grieve, let us also rejoice that we had the joy of knowing _____ and remember that we would not trade away that joy even to escape this sadness.

Facilitator:

In order to cope with death, we must reaffirm our understanding that each of our lives has a purpose that transcends this physical existence. Let us recite together the poem "Solace" by Susan Mumm:

Solace

A human being
I am born,
knowing not my origins,
knowing not my fate.
Yet these things I know.
I am part of
a larger whole.
Though someday
I shall die,
In fact,
I am immortal.
For I am part
of
all that came before me,
And all
that shall come after.
I
am
a link
in the ever-evolving
family
of all people.
Though I shall
die,
the gifts I give
to others,
shall live on.
All that I give
of myself,
--the love that helps
others to
manifest their full potential,
And the
bits of knowledge
I add
to the collective wisdom,
Shall contribute
to the welfare
of
humanity
to come.

```
                    I
                   am
                a seed
                   of
                Nature,
            Through which
                  life
                 passes
                  from
                   one
                    to
                another,
                   in
              never-ending
                growth.
         In this
              knowledge
                   I
                 find
                  joy
                   in
               existence,
                 and
                  solace
                   in
                 death.
```

Susan M. Mumm

Facilitator:

Let us each take a few moments to share with each other the gifts that _____ has given each of us in his/her lifetime.

(This sharing is probably best done sitting in a circle. Allow ample time for each person to speak for a few minutes. Crying should not be discouraged; it is part of the grieving process.)

Facilitator:

May we now join hands and offer a prayer of thanks to _____ for the gifts s/he has given us.

Facilitator and Guests:
   (In Unison)

_____, we thank you for the precious gifts you have given us. A part of you shall live on in us.

Facilitator starts music.

Facilitator:

As we face death again, we are reminded of our own impending deaths. Let us take this opportunity to remind ourselves to live our lives such that we can approach our own deaths with calmness and serenity. May we all leave here today with a renewed commitment to become more loving and giving human beings, that we may in our unique ways, help humankind grow to its fullest heights.

(**Pause**)

Facilitator:

_____ has donated his/her body to ___(name of institution)___ for medical research, so that his/her death will help the living.

Facilitator:

_____ will now read a sonnet by John Masefield for the closing reading.

Reader:

> _It may be so with us, that in the dark,_
> _When we have done with Time and wander Space,_
> _Some meeting of the blind may strike a spark,_
> _And to Death's empty mansion give a grace._
>
> _It may be, that the loosened soul may find_
> _Some new delight of living without limbs,_
> _Bodiless joy of flesh-untrammeld mind,_
> _Peace like a sky where starlike spirit swims._
>
> _It may be, that the million cells of sense,_
> _Loosed from their seventy years' adhesion, pass_
> _Each to some joy changed experience,_
> _Weight in the earth or glory in the grass;_
>
> _It may be that we cease; we cannot tell._
> _Yet even if we cease, life is a miracle._

> _Reprinted with permission of Macmillan Publishing Company, from The Poems of John Masefield by John Masefield, Copyright 1916 by Macmillan Publishing Company, renewed 1944 by John Masefield._

Facilitator:

The family wishes to thank everyone for attending. The ceremony is ended. Go in peace.

Outline for Designing and Facilitating an Alternative Funeral Service

I. Introduction by Person Chosen to Be Facilitator:

This should be a brief outline of what will happen at the service--the purpose of coming together for a funeral. My rationale here is that it makes sense to use the same general rules you would use for any group meeting. The general rule of thumb is to always start meetings with a statement of the purpose of the meeting and an explanation of what participants can expect to happen.

II. Acknowledgement of Grief, and Statement about Inevitability and Purpose of Grief:

Verbally acknowledging the grief that everyone is feeling is a means of pulling everyone together, of helping them to feel emotionally close. Talking about grief as an inevitable part of human existence that everyone goes through will help people feel more confident that they will be able to cope and pick up the pieces. The pain can feel very overwhelming and frightening. Discussing the positive aspects of sadness, i.e., re-asserting that joy cannot exist without pain, is consoling.

III. Renewal/Affirmation that Death Has a Divine Purpose:

(Note: In an atheist service you would instead relate death as being part of the cycle of Nature.)

Because death is such an intensely sad and frightening time, a renewal in God, an after-life, a Divine plan, etc., are key components in a funeral. It is important to help people view their immediate experience with death in a broader perspective; to enable them to see death as necessary to attain a greater end. Viewing death from this perspective makes their pain more bearable because death is seen as having an important purpose. Often people who are not normally very religious feel a strong need to feel connected to God and to feel themselves to be part of a Divine plan when faced with the death of a loved one.

There are obviously an infinite amount of poems, and readings that can be used for this part of the service. The selection should be based on the wishes of the deceased and the needs of the people attending the funeral. If there is a great deal of difference in the religious beliefs of family and friends of the deceased, it often makes sense to have several different selections read. In extreme cases it may make most sense to hold dual services, each one being tailored to the religious preferences of those attending. There is a list of suggested readings and poems on at the end of this chapter.

IV. Playing of Selected Music:

"Music is the language of the soul." Thus, music is an integral part of any funeral. I have often heard people say that a given piece of music can move them more than any words. I think music is particularly helpful at funerals because it often captures the ebb and flow of life. The notes flow together to form a harmonious whole, just as life and death flow together and blend into the whole of human existence. People often use music that was particularly liked by the deceased.

V. Expression of Gratitude to the Deceased for Gifts Given in His/Her Lifetime, and Prayers of Love and Encouragement to the Deceased in His/Her New Realm of Existence:

(Allow Ample Time for This)

This part of the ceremony replaces the traditional eulogy. It allows for participation by everyone attending the funeral, an aspect, that I think is seriously lacking from traditional funerals. Each person attending the funeral is given the opportunity to speak about the gifts the deceased has given them in his/her lifetime.* Being of a more personal nature than a traditional eulogy, it can bring to light not just the obvious accomplishments of the deceased person's life, but also the more subtle ways he/she enriched and transformed the lives of people he/she touched during his/her lifetime. This sharing helps people to reaffirm that those who have died go on enriching our lives far beyond the time they are alive.

This exercise can also serve as an inspiration to those participating, to draw closer to their family and friends. By hearing how the deceased person's life touched the souls of those he/she left behind, participants recognize more fully how important their relationships with one another are. In addition, there are many people who believe that the spirit of the deceased is present at the funeral. So this sharing may also serve the purpose of clarifying for the deceased person how they were viewed in their life by others. Lastly, joining together to verbally send encouragement to the deceased is a tradition that has been part of funeral rituals for thousands of years. It helps to reaffirm that the life of the spirit exists beyond death. Prayers of love and encouragement voiced as a group create an amazing positive energy.

VI. Acknowledgement of What Death Can Teach the Living:

I've sat through many a fire and brimstone funeral service with the preacher taking full advantage of a captive audience to implore each and every one in the audience to take Jesus into their hearts right then and there, because death could get them at any time. I do not advocate proselytizing at funerals. However, death does in fact carry an inherent message for the living: that we are mortal and need to evaluate whether we are living our lives as we most want to be living them. I think that a brief, nurturing statement about using this death as a catalyst to make the changes we long to make in our own lives is useful.

VII. Closing Announcements:

1) Thank people for attending.

---

*Several people have asked me, "What if someone famous died and there were thousands of people at the funeral?"
My suggestion is to break into sub-groups of twenty people each, for this exercise.

2) If burial will follow the service, an announcement should be made for last viewing of the casket. Also announce whether the grave-side service will be for family only, or open to everyone. Announce where the deceased will be buried--this is useful for people who may want to visit the grave later.

3) If the deceased's body has been cremated, make an announcement regarding the interment or scattering of the ashes. If the deceased requested that his/her ashes be scattered somewhere in particular, that should be announced.

Examples:

a) "Since John loved the mountains, his wife will scatter his ashes in Rocky Mountain National Park."

b) "Mary has requested that her ashes be scattered in the Mississippi River for she firmly believed that as rivers flow onward so shall her spirit."

4) If the deceased has donated his/her body for scientific research, announce that.

VIII. Closing Reading:

This should be something brief. Since these parting words will be what remain freshest in people's minds, I suggest trying to include some specific ideas to help them cope with their grief. E.g., "Let us remember, in the coming months, to share our grief with one another, for sadness is always made more bearable by sharing it with the people we are closest to."

IX. Closing Statement:

Finalize the service so that people know it has ended and so the service does not end on a abrupt note. E.g., "The service is ended. Go in peace."

X. Grave-side Service (If Applicable):

I suggest that this be kept fairly brief. People are often cold or hot, exhausted, and the children are restless by this point.

You may want to consider filling in the grave as part of the service. These days, this is rare; the casket is usually lowered and the grave closed after the people leave. However, in former days, the grave was, of course, filled in by the family and friends. I think the fact that family and friends no longer participate in closing the grave encourages people to avoid dealing with death, rather than acknowledging and working through their grief surrounding death. I almost had to laugh at the explanation given to me by a funeral director when I asked him why those attending the funeral no longer participate in the closing of the grave: "It's too emotional. It makes people cry." How absurd! Death is emotional, and crying is a healthy human response to sadness! The purpose of a funeral is to provide a supportive environment in which to grieve. The more crying and grieving that can be done at the grave side, the less that will have to be done in the months that follow. Most cemeteries will allow family and friends to at least be present and throw handfuls of dirt, though some will require that the cemetery staff do the major part. You may be able to find a cemetery that will allow you to do the entire grave closing yourself. If participating is important to you, make sure you inquire beforehand, and choose a cemetery that will allow you this freedom.

Putting Your Instructions for the Type of Funeral You Would Like in Writing

At this point, you are familiar with the laws regarding funeral arrangements. You have examined the pros and cons for various methods of body disposition and you have a lot of ideas swimming in your head about options for funeral services. It is finally time to put all you've learned into writing. Below is a sample "Letter of Instruction Regarding My Funeral Arrangements." I suggest you take some time filling this out. Write a draft, and then put it away for a month and bring it back out and see if it still feels right. Also encourage other members of your family to complete their own letters of instruction.

Please keep in mind that the requests you make regarding your funeral arrangements both in terms of body disposition and funeral/memorial service are not legally binding (see pages 56-66). However, putting your preferences in writing will make your preferences known to your surviving kin, and will increase the chances that your wishes will be held up in court if there is a dispute regarding your funeral arrangements.

Letter of Instruction Regarding My Funeral Arrangements

Your full name: _____

Date: _____

GENERAL

1) List the person you would like to be in charge of making your funeral arrangements: _____

2) List family, friends, and acquaintances you would like informed of your death, and where their phone numbers are filed:

3) List particular information you would like included in your obituary, e.g. specific accomplishments:

4) List any requests about cost of funeral:

5) List any insurance policy you have, or money set aside, to cover costs of funeral and where policy papers/money are located:

6) List any other relevant information:

DISPOSITION OF BODY

1) Burial

   a) Do you have a preference for a particular cemetery?

   b) Do you own a grave lot there?

2) Entombment

   a) Do you have a preference for a particular columbarium?

   b) Do you own a space there?

3) Cremation

   a) Do you wish your ashes to be scattered?

      1) Where?

      2) By Whom?

   b) Do you prefer your ashes to be buried or entombed?

      1) Where?

c) Would you like your ashes given to a particular person?

Ashes to be given to: _____

4) Donation of Body for Scientific Research

a) Do you have a preference for a particular school, hospital, etc.?

b) Have you made any pre-arrangements to donate your body to a specific organization? If so, where are the documents specifying your wishes?

SERVICE

1) Do you want your body to be present at the funeral/memorial service?

2) Do you want an open or closed casket?

3) Do you wish to: be embalmed?   not be embalmed?

4) Do you prefer flowers or donations to memorial funds?
What organization(s) should memorial funds be donated to?

5) Do you want your funeral service to be facilitated by a clergy person?
If so, who? _____
Do you prefer for a friend/relative to facilitate?
If so, who? _____

6) List particular people you would like given the opportunity to speak at your service:

7) List particular selections you would like read at your funeral (poems, a personal statement from you, spiritual/religious readings):

8) List anything you might want omitted from your funeral, e.g., mention of God if you are an atheist:

9) List any particular music you would like played at your service:

10) Where would you like the service held (church, funeral home, residence, other)?

11) List people you would like to serve as pallbearers. (Consider women, too, of course!).

12) Additional comments:

Signature: _____

Notarization: _____

_____

Author's Note:

This "Letter of Instruction Regarding My Funeral Arrangements" may be reproduced, despite the fact that it is copyrighted, provided it is for personal use, or for use by non-profit groups.

Discussing Your Letter of Instruction with Family and Other Relevant People

After you have put your wishes regarding your funeral arrangements into writing, it is extremely important to discuss them with family and other relevant people. I cannot stress the importance of this enough. As you know from reading the sections in this chapter about the laws governing funeral arrangements, there is no legislation which binds your surviving kin to carry through your express wishes, even if you have them outlined in a written, notarized document. Thus, if they oppose what you are requesting, they can try to override your wishes. By discussing matters beforehand, you can hopefully come to an agreement and the case will not end up in court. Particularly, if you are requesting arrangements that might upset your kin (e.g. if they oppose cremation and you are requesting that, or if they would want a religious service and you are requesting a secular one), it's better to break this news to them before your death. You will then have the opportunity to explain your reasons and hear their misgivings and you can probably come up with something that both of you feel comfortable with. When bringing up the matter of funeral arrangements, make sure that you choose a time that is convenient and conducive to such a serious topic.

If you can not reach agreement with your family after your discussions, you should probably appoint a friend, who is sympathetic to your preferences regarding your funeral, to be in charge of your funeral arrangements. As you know from reading the sections on funeral law, this appointed person would have no guaranteed authority to take care of your funeral arrangements. However, he/she could represent you in probate court, if your family tried to overrule your wishes regarding funeral arrangements. Make sure this friend has a notarized copy of your letter of instruction.

Of course, in the meantime, you should be very active in trying to get legislation passed which will guarantee individuals the right to determine their own funeral arrangements. Don't forget to send in the legislative package included in this chapter.

Getting Your Letter of Instruction Regarding Funeral Arrangements Notarized

After you have arrived at the final draft of your letter of instruction regarding funeral arrangements, and you've shown it to your family, get your document notarized. If your family disagrees with your requests for funeral arrangements, your requests need to be notarized so that your wishes are more likely to be upheld by the court, (if it comes to that). However, even if your family is sympathetic to your wishes, it is good policy to have a notarized document. You may, through the years, state different preferences to different members of the family. By having one notarized, your family will know that the preferences you wrote down are the ones you ultimately decided upon. I would suggest having two copies at least, both notarized. Keep one for yourself, and give one to the person you want to make your funeral arrangements. Make sure several people know where your copy is filed in case the others get lost. If you make any changes in the future, make sure to get it re-notarized and inform your family and relevant others of any changes.

Additional Readings

For

Alternative Funeral/Memorial Services

My friend, listen now, for that which is called death has arrived. So let go gently, gently, of all that holds you back. Of all that pulls you away from this most precious moment. Know that now you have arrived at the transition called death. Open to it. Let go into it.

Recognize the changing experience of the mind as it separates from the body, dissolving.

Dissolving now into the realms of pure light. Your true nature shining everywhere before you.

My friend, the clear light of your original nature is revealed now in this release from heavier form. Enter into the brilliance of the light. Approach it with reverence and compassion. Draw it into yourself and become what you have always been.

My friend, maintain an openheartedness, a spaciousness of being that does not grasp. Let things be as they are without the least attempt to interfere. Pushing away nothing. Grasping at nothing.

Enter the essential nature of your own being shining there before you, a great luminosity. Rest in being. Knowing it for what it is. This light shining, luminous. Your true self.

My friend, at this moment your mind is pure luminous emptiness. Your original mind, the essence of being, shines before you. Its nature is compassion and love, vibrant and luminous.

...Let go, gently, gently, without the least force. Before you shines your true being. It is without birth, without death. It is the immortal light seen shining in the eyes of newborns. Recognize this. It is the Evershining.

Let go of all which distracts or confuses the mind, all that created density in life. Let go into your undifferentiated nature shining there before you. You have always been this light now revealed.

Go gently into it. Do not be frightened or bewildered. Do not pull back in fear from the immensity of your true being. Now is a moment for liberation.

...Listen without distraction, for what is called death has arrived. You are not alone in leaving this world. It happens to everyone. Do not desire or yearn for the body you have just left behind. You cannot stay. Indeed to force back into this life will only cause you to wander in bewilderment and confusion, stumbling in the illusions of the mind. Painting wonders that do not exist. Creating terrors that are unreal. Open to the truth. Trust in your own great nature.

...Now is the time for holding nowhere, for melting into the great light of your original nature. Melt, dissolve into the luminosity of being.

...Go forward. Stay nowhere in mind, letting all that arises pass away as it does.

...Float free in the vast spaciousness. Your devotion to the truth will carry you through.

...Move with devotion and openheartedness towards the light. Become the pure edgeless spaciousness within which the flow continues.

My friend, many days have passed now since you left your body. Now know the truth as it is and go on, taking refuge in the vastness of your original nature. Know that you are well guided by your compassion and love. You are the essence of all things. You are the light.

Stephen Levine, <u>Who Dies? An Investigation of Conscious Living and Conscious Dying</u>, Copyright 1982 by Stephen Levine. Reprinted with permission of Doubleday & Company Inc., New York, pp. 284, 285, 286, 289.

Darest Thou Now O Soul

Darest thou now, O Soul,
Walk out with me toward the unknown region,
Where neither ground is for the feet nor any path to follow?

No map there, nor guide,
Nor voice sounding, nor touch of human hand,
Nor face with blooming flesh, nor lips, nor eyes, are in that land.

I know it not O Soul,
Nor dost thou, all is a blank before us,
All waits, undream'd of in that region, that inaccessible land.

Till, when the ties loosen,
All but the ties eternal, Time and Space,
Nor darkness, gravitation, sense, nor any bounds bounding us.

Then we burst forth, we float,
In Time and Space O Soul, prepared for them,
Equal, equipt at last, (O Joy! O fruit of all!) them to fulfil O soul.

Walt Whitman, Leaves of Grass

98

Come lovely and soothing death,
Undulate round the world, serenely arriving, arriving,
In the day, in the night, to all, to each,
Sooner or later delicate death.

Prais'd be the fathomless universe,
For life and joy, and for objects and knowledge curious,
And for love, sweet love--but praise! praise! praise!
For the sure-enwinding arms of cool-enfolding death.

Dark mother always gliding near with soft feet,
Have none chanted for thee a chant of fullest welcome?
Then I chant it for thee, I glorify thee above all,
I bring thee a song that when thou must indeed come, come unfalteringly.

Approach strong deliveress,
When it is so, when thou hast taken them I joyously sing the dead,
Lost in the loving floating ocean of thee,
Laved in the flood of thy bliss O death.

From me to thee glad serenades,
Dances for thee I propose saluting thee, adornments and feastings for thee,
And the sights of the open landscape and the high-spread sky are fitting,
And life and the fields, and the huge and thoughtful night.

The night in silence under many a star,
The ocean shore and the husky whispering wave whose voice I know,
And the soul turning to thee O vast and well-veil'd death,
And the body gratefully nestling close to thee.

Over the tree-tops I float thee a song,
Over the rising and sinking waves, over the myriad fields and the prairies wide,
Over the dense-pack'd cities all and the teeming wharves and ways,
I float this carol with joy, with joy to thee O death.

Walt Whitman, <u>Leaves Of Grass</u>.

Assurances

I need no assurances, I am a man who is preoccupied of his own soul;
I do not doubt that from under the feet and beside the hands and face
        I am cognizant of, are now looking faces I am not cognizant of,
        calm and actual faces,
I do not doubt but the majesty and beauty of the world are latent
        in any iota of the world,
I do not doubt I am limitless, and that the universes are limitless,
        in vain I try to think how limitless,
I do not doubt the orbs and the systems of orbs play their swift sports
        through the air on purpose, and that I shall one day be eligible
        to do as much as they, and more than they,
I do not doubt that temporary affairs keep on and on millions of years,
I do not doubt interiors have their interiors, and exteriors have their exteriors,
        and that the eyesight has another eyesight, and the hearing
        another hearing, and the voice another voice,
I do not doubt that the passionately-wept deaths of young men are provided
        for, and that deaths of young women and the deaths
        of little children are provided for,
(Did you think Life was so well provided for, and Death,
        the purport of all Life, is not well provided for?)
I do not doubt that wrecks at sea, no matter what the horrors of them,
        no matter whose wife, child, husband, father, lover, has gone down,
        are provided for, to the minutest points,
I do not doubt that whatever can possibly happen anywhere at any time,
        is provided for in the inherences of things,
I do not think Life provides for all and for Time and Space,
        but I believe Heavenly Death provides for all.

Walt Whitman, <u>Leaves of Grass</u>.

There is no need to be afraid of death. It is not the end of the physical body that should worry us. Rather, our concern must be to <u>live</u> while we're alive--to release our inner selves from the spiritual death that comes with living behind a facade designed to conform to external definitions of who and what we are. Every individual human being born on this earth has the capacity to become a unique and special person unlike any who has ever existed before or will ever exist again. But to the extent that we become captives of culturally defined role expectations and behaviors--stereotypes, not ourselves,--we block our capacity for self-actualization. We interfere with our becoming all that we can be.

Death is the key to the door of life. It is through accepting the finiteness of our individual existences that we are enabled to find the strength and courage to reject those extrinsic roles and expectations and to devote each day of our lives--however long they may be--to growing as fully as we are able. We must learn to draw on our inner resources, to define ourselves in terms of the feedback we receive from our own internal valuing system rather than trying to fit ourselves into some illfitting stereotyped role.

It is the denial of death that is partially responsible for people living empty, purposeless lives; for when you live as if you'll live forever, it becomes too easy to postpone the things you know that you must do. You live your life in preparation for tomorrow or in remembrance of yesterday, and meanwhile, each today is lost. In contrast, when you fully understand that each day you awaken could be the last you have, you take the time <u>that day</u> to grow, to become more of who you really are, to reach out to other human beings.

There is an urgency that each of you, no matter how many days or weeks or months or years you have to live, commit yourself to growth. We are living in a time of uncertainty, anxiety, fear, and despair. It is essential that you become aware of the light, power, and strength within each of you, and that you learn to use those inner resources in service of your own and others' growth. The world is in desperate need of human beings whose own level of growth is sufficient to enable them to learn to live and work with others cooperatively and lovingly, to care for others--not for what those others can do for you or for what they think of you, but rather in terms of what you can do for them. If you send forth love to others, you will receive in return the reflection of that love; because of your loving behavior, you will grow, and you will shine a light that will brighten the darkness of the time we live in--whether it is in a sickroom of a dying patient, on the corner of a ghetto street in Harlem, or in your own home.

Humankind will survive only through the commitment and involvement of individuals in their own and others' growth and development as human beings. This means development of loving and caring relationships in which all members are as committed to the growth and happiness of the others as they are to their own. Through commitment to personal growth individual human beings will also make their contribution to the growth and development--the evolution--of the whole species to become all that humankind can and is meant to be. Death is the key to that evolution. For only when we understand the real meaning of death to human existence will we have the courage to become what we are destined to be.

When human beings understand their place in the universe, they will become able to grow to assume that place. But the answer is not in words on this page. The answer is within you. You can become a channel and a source of great inner strength. But you must give up everything in order to gain everything. What must you give up? All that is not truly you; all that you have chosen without choosing and value without evaluating, accepting because of someone else's extrinsic judgement, rather than your own; all your self-doubt that keeps you from trusting and loving yourself or other human beings. What will you gain? Only your own, true self; a self who is at peace, who is able to truly love and be loved, and who understands who and what (s)he is meant for. But you can be yourself only if you are no one else. You must give up "their" approval, whoever, they are, and look to yourself for evaluation of success and failure, in terms of your own level of aspiration that is consistent with your values. Nothing is simpler and nothing is more difficult.

Where can you find the strength and courage to reject those outer definitions of yourself and choose, instead, your own?

It is all within you if you look and are not afraid. Death can show us the way, for when we know and understand completely that our time on this earth is limited, and that we have no way of knowing when it will be over, then we must live each day as if it were the only one we had. We must take the time, now, to begin--one step at a time, at a pace that makes us not afraid, but rather eager, to take the next step, to grow into ourselves. If you practice life with compassion, love, courage, patience, hope, and faith, you will be rewarded by an ever increasing consciousness of the help that can come forth if only you look within yourself for strength and guidance. When human beings "find a place of stillness and quiet at the highest level of which they are capable, then the heavenly influences can pour into them, recreate them, and use them for the salvation of humankind."

Death is the final stage of growth in this life. There is no total death. Only the body dies. The self or spirit, or whatever you may wish to label it, is eternal. You may interpret this in any way that makes you comfortable.

If you wish, you may view the eternal essence of your existence in terms of the impact your every mood and action has on those you touch, and then in turn, on those they touch, and on and on--even long after your life span is completed. You will never know, for example, the rippling effects of the smile and words of encouragement you give to other human beings with whom you come in contact.

You may be more comfortable and comforted by a faith that there is a source of goodness, light, and strength greater than any of us individually, yet still within us all, and that each essential self has an existence that transcends the finiteness of the physical and contributes to that greater power.

Death, in this context, may be viewed as the curtain between the existence that we are conscious of and one that is hidden from us until we raise that curtain. Whether we open it symbolically in order to understand the finiteness, of the existence we know, thus learning to live each day the best we can, or whether we open it in actuality when we end that physical existence is not the issue. What is important is to realize that whether we understand fully why we are here or what will happen when we die, it is our purpose as human beings to grow--to look within ourselves to find and build upon that source of peace and understanding and strength which is our inner selves, and to reach out to others with love, acceptance, patient guidance, and hope for what we may all become together.

In order to be at peace, it is necessary to feel a sense of history--that you are both part of what has come before and part of what is yet to come. Being thus surrounded, you are not alone; and the sense of urgency that pervades the present is put in perspective: Do not frivolously use the time that is yours to spend. Cherish it, that each day may bring new growth, insight, and awareness. Use this growth not selfishly, but rather in service of what may be, in the future tide of time. Never allow a day to pass that did not add to what was understood before. Let each day be a stone in the path of growth. Do not rest until what was intended has been done. But remember--go as slowly as is necessary in order to sustain a steady pace; do not expend energy in waste. Finally, do not allow the illusory urgencies of the immediate to distract you from your vision of the eternal...

Elizabeth Kubler-Ross, Laurie Braga, and Joesph Braga, Death: The Final State of Growth, Prentice-Hall, Englewood Cliffs, New Jersey, 1975, pp. 164-167

...Death opens the door to life, to life renewed and re-experienced as a child experiences it, with the dew still on it.

And so comes the next opening--the sense of being part of a universe, of a personal relatedness to all life, all growth, all creativity. Suddenly one senses that his life is not just his own little individual existence, but that he is bound in fact to all of life, from the first splitting off of the planets, through the beginning of animate life and on through the slow evolution of man. It is all in him and he is but one channel of it. What has flowed through him [her], flows on, through children, through works accomplished, through services rendered; it is not lost. Once given the vision of one's true place in the life stream, death is no longer complete or final, but an incident. Death is the way--the only way--life renews itself. When the individual has served his purpose as a channel, the flow transfers itself to other channels, but life goes on. And in this great drama of life renewed, one sees and feels the divine presence, and feels himself one with it.

Bradford Smith, <u>Dear Gift Of Life: A Man's Encounter With Death</u>, Pendle Hill Pamphlet 142 (Wallingford, PA: Pendle Hill Publications) 1965, p. 15, Reprinted with permission.

Madonna Natura   (Mother Nature)

I love and worship thee in that thy ways
Are fair, and that the glory of past days
   Haloes thy brightness with a sacred hue.
Within thine eyes are dreams of mystic things,
Within thy voice a subtler music rings
   Than ever mortal from the keen reeds drew;
Thou weav'st a web which men have called Death
But Life is in the magic of thy breath.

The secret things of Earth thou knowest well;
Thou seest the wild bee build his narrow cell,
   The lonely eagle wing through lonely skies,
The lion on the desert roam afar,
The glow-worm glitter like a fallen star,
   The hour-lived insect as it hums and flies;
Thou seest men like shadows come and go,
And all their endless dreams drift to and fro.

In thee is strength, endurance, wisdom, truth;
Thou art above all mortal joy and ruth,
   Thou hast the calm and silence of the night;
Mayhap thou seest what we cannot see,
Surely far off thou hear'st harmoniously
   Echoes of flawless music infinite,
Mayhap thou feel'st thrilling through each sod
Beneath thy feet the very breath of God.

Monna Natura, fair and grand and great,
I worship thee, who art inviolate:
   Through thee I reach to things beyond this span
Of mine own puny life, through thee I learn
Courage and hope, and dimly can discern
   The ever noble grades awaiting man [humanity]:
Madonna, unto thee I bend and pray--
Saviour, Redeemer thou, whom none can slay!

No human fanes are dedicate to thee,
But thine the temples of each tameless sea,
   Each mountain height and forest glade and plain:
No priests with daily hymns thy praises sing,
But far and wide the wild winds chanting swing,
   And dirge the sea waves on the changeless main,
While songs of birds fill all the fields and woods
And cries of beasts the savage solitudes.

Hearken, Madonna, hearken to my cry;
Teach me through metaphors of liberty,
    Till strong and fearing nought in life or death
I feel thy sacred freedom through me thrill,
Wise, and defiant, with unquenched will
    Unyielding, though succumb the mortal breath--
Then if I conquer, take me by the hand
And guide me onward to thy Promised Land!

William Sharp   (Pen-name Fiona Macleod)

"Listen, my friend! I am a sinner and you are a sinner, but someday the sinner will be Brahma again, will someday attain Nirvana, will someday become a Buddha. Now this "someday" is illusion; it is only a comparison. The sinner is not on the way to a Buddha-like state; he is not evolving, although our thinking cannot conceive things otherwise. No, the potential Buddha already exists in the sinner; his future is already there. The potential hidden Buddha must be recognized in him, in you, in everybody. The world, Govinda, is not imperfect or slowly evolving along a long path to perfection. No, it is perfect at every moment; every sin already carries grace within it, all small children are potential old men, all sucklings have death within them, all dying people--eternal life. It is not possible for one person to see how far another is on the way; the Buddha exists in the robber and dice player; the robber exists in the Brahmin. During deep meditation it is possible to dispel time, to see simultaneously all the past, present and future, and then everything is good, everything is perfect, everything is Brahman. Therefore it seems to me that everything that exists is good--death as well as life, sin as well as holiness, wisdom as well as folly. Everything is necessary, everything needs only my agreement, my assent, my loving understanding; then all is well with me and nothing can harm me."

". . . Bend near to me!" he whispered in Govinda's ear. "Come, still nearer, quite close! Kiss me on the forehead, Govinda."

Although surprised, Govinda was compelled by a great love and presentiment to obey him; he leaned close to him and touched his forehead with his lips. As he did this, something wonderful happened to him. While he was still dwelling on Siddhartha's strange words, while he strove in vain to dispel the conception of time, to imagine Nirvana and Samsara as one, while even a certain contempt for his friend's words conflicted with a tremendous love and esteem for him, this happened to him.

He no longer saw the face of his friend Siddhartha. Instead he saw other faces, many faces, a long series, a continuous stream of faces--hundreds, thousands, which all came and disappeared and yet all seemed to be there at the same time, which all continually changed and renewed themselves and which were yet all Siddhartha. He saw the face of a fish, of a carp, with tremendous painfully opened mouth, a dying fish with dimmed eyes. He saw the face of a newly born child, red and full of wrinkles, ready to cry. He saw the face of a murderer, saw him plunge a knife into the body of a man; at the same moment he saw this criminal kneeling down, bound, and his head cut off by an executioner. He saw the naked bodies of men and women in the postures and transports of passionate love. He saw corpses stretched out, still, cold, empty. He saw the heads of animals--boars, crocodiles, elephants, oxen, birds. He saw Krishna and Agni. He saw all these forms and faces in a thousand relationships to each other, all helping each other, loving, hating and destroying each other and become newly born. Each one was mortal, a passionate, painful example of all that is transitory. Yet none of them died, they only changed, were always reborn, continually had a new face: only time stood between one face and another. And all these forms and faces rested, flowed, reproduced, swam past and merged into each other, and over them all there was continually something thin, unreal and yet existing, stretched across like thin glass or ice, like a transparent skin, shell, form or mask of water--and this mask was Siddhartha's smiling face which Govinda touched with his lips at that moment. And Govinda saw that this mask-like smile, this smile of unity over the flowing forms, this smile of simultaneousness over the thousands of births and deaths--this smile of Siddhartha--was exactly the same as the calm, delicate, impenetrable, perhaps gracious, perhaps mocking, wise, thousand-fold smile of Gotama the Buddha, as he perceived it with awe a hundred times. . . .

Hermann Hesse, _Siddhartha,_ Copyright 1951 by New Directions Publishing Corporation, pp. 143, 144, 149, 150, 151. Reprinted with permission.

When They Remember Me

Friends would gather.
    Choosing night. Knowing my love of it.
Each person bringing a food to
    share, a drink to warm.
Bringing it to the outdoors, gathering
    together in the wild,
      gathering near water,
        gathering under the cover of green,
      gathering wood for a fire,
        gathering strength, joining hands.

    Circling with love, upon the land
      calling me to mind.
    Naming me to the wind.
    Sending me to the Goddess.
      Releasing me to the unknown.
    Calling out to the ancients to the directions.

    Noises in throats, warmth in the belly.
    Cries in the lungs, tears in the eyes.
      Letting me go.
        Letting me know.
    Knowing the weakness of our strength.
    The strength of our weakness.

Someone would move, moving others.
    Someone would laugh, loving others.
Someone would cry, needing others.
    Someone would sing, healing others.
      Someone would talk, soothing others.

    Hands would be joined.
      Feet would be free.
Knowing the earth, sensing the sky.
      Knowing my spirit to fly.
There would be dancing.
There would be cleansing.
      There would be loving.
There would be grounding.
There would be silence.
    There,
      would be me.

Julia Bayha, Unpublished poem.
Reprinted with Permission

Last Lines

  No coward soul is mine,
No trembler in the world's storm-troubled sphere:
  I see Heaven's glories shine,
And faith shines equal, arming me from fear.

  O God, within my breast,
Almighty, ever-present Deity!
  Life--that in me has rest,
As I--undying Life--have power in Thee!

  Vain are the thousand creeds
That move men's hearts: unutterably vain;
  Worthless as withered weeds,
Or idlest froth amid the boundless main,

  To waken doubt in one
Holding so fast by thine infinity;
  So surely anchored on
The steadfast rock of immortality.

  With wide-embracing love
Thy Spirit animates eternal years,
  Pervades and broods above,
Changes, sustains, dissolves, creates, and rears.

  Though earth and man were gone,
And suns and universes ceased to be,
  And Thou were left alone,
Every existence would exist in Thee.

  There is not room for Death,
Nor atom that his might could render void:
  Thou--Thou art Being and Breath,
And what Thou art may never be destroyed.

    Emily Bronte

Those I would teach; and by right reason bring
To think of death as but an idle thing.
Why thus affrightened at an empty name,
A dream of darkness, and fictitious flame...
What feels the body when the soul expires,
By time corrupted, or consumed by fires?
...the spirit, but new life repeats
In other form, and only changes seats.

...Then death, so call'd, is but old matter dress'd
In some new figure, and a varied vest:
Thus all things are but alter'd, nothing dies;
And here and there the unbodied spirit flies....
From tenement to tenement though toss'd,
The soul is still the same, the figure only lost:

And as the soften'd wax new seals receives,
This face assumes, and that impression leaves:
Now call'd by one, now by another name;
The form is only changed, the wax is still the same,
So death, so call'd, can but the form deface,
The immortal soul flies out in empty space;
To seek her fortune in some other place.

Ovid

Taken From <u>*Poetical Works of John Dryden*</u> *London*
1886 IV, pp. 292-93.

The Eternal Springtime

Remember, in the darkening hour, that the glow of the universe once filled thy heart, and that thou hast acknowledged the magnitude of existence. Hast thou not looked forth into one half of infinity by night, and into the other half by day? Think away the nothingness of space and the earth which is around thee; worlds above, around and beneath, arch thee about as a center, all impelling and impelled; splendor within splendor, magnitude within magnitude; all brightness centering in the universal sun. Carry thy thoughts forward through eternity towards that universal sun; thou shalt not arrive at darkness nor emptiness. What is empty dwells only between the worlds, not around the world....

Remember, in the dark hour, how in the spring of thy life the mounds of earth which are graves, appeared to thee only as the mountain tops of another far and new world; and how, in the midst of the fulness of life, thou didst acknowledge the value of death. The snow of the grave shall warm the frost-bitten limbs of age to life again. As a navigator who suddenly disembarks from the cold, wintry and lonely sea, upon a coast which is laden with the warm rich blossoms of spring, so with one leap from our little bark we pass at once from winter to an eternal springtime.

Rejoice in this dark hour that thy life dwells in the midst of a wider and larger life. The earth clod of the globe has been divinely breathed upon. A world swarms with life, for the leaf of every tree is a land of souls; and every little life would freeze and perish if it was not warmed and borne up by the eddies of life about it. The sea of time glitters, like the sea of space, with countless beings of light, death and resurrection on the valleys and mountains of the ever-swelling ocean....

Never forget the thought, which is now so clear to thee, that the individuality of man [humanity] lasts out the greatest suffering and the most entrancing joy alike unscathed, while the body crumbles away in the pains and pleasures of the flesh. Herein are souls like marsh lights, which shine in the storms and the rain unextinguishable.

Jean Paul Richter

Readings From The Bhagavad Gita

Adapted by Susan Mumm

The wise grieve not for those who live; and they grieve not for those who die--for life and death shall pass away.

Because we all have been for all time. And we all shall be for all time, we all for ever and ever.

As the spirit of our mortal body wanders on in childhood, and youth and old age, the Spirit wanders on to a new body: of this the sage has no doubts.

Interwoven in creation, the Spirit is beyond destruction.
No one can bring to an end the Spirit which is everlasting.

For beyond time the Spirit dwells in these bodies, though these bodies have an end in their time; but the Spirit remains immeasurable, immortal.

The eternal Spirit cannot die. The Spirit is never born, and never dies. It is in eternity and is for evermore. Never-born and eternal, beyond times gone or to come, the Spirit does not die when the body dies.

As one leaves an old garment and puts on one that is new, the Spirit leaves the mortal body and then puts on one that is new.

Weapons cannot hurt the Spirit and fire can never burn. Untouched by drenching waters, untouched by parching winds, the Spirit is everlasting, omni-present, never-changing, never-moving, ever One.

The Spirit that is in all beings is immortal in them all: for the death of what cannot die, cease thou to sorrow.

As I accepted the change of the golden hair of my childhood to the reddish-brown hair of my youth without regret, so I also accept my silver hair--and I am ready to accept the time when my hair and the rest of my clay garment returns to the dust from which it came, while my spirit goes on to freer living. It is the season for my hair to be silver, and each season has its lessons to teach. Each season of life is wonderful if you have learned the lessons of the season before. It is only when you go on with lessons unlearned that you wish for a return.

...If we but knew how short is the earth life in comparison with the whole, we would be less troubled with the difficulties of the earth life than we are troubled now with the difficulties of one of our days...

Peace Pilgrim, Peace Pilgrim: Her Life And Work In Her Own Words, Ocean Tree Books, Santa Fe, New Mexico, 1983, pp. 84, 85.

Faith

I will not doubt, though all my ships at sea
    Come drifting home with broken masts and sails;
    I shall believe the Hand which never fails,
From seeming evil worketh good to me;
    And, though I weep because those sails are battered,
    Still will I cry, while my best hopes lie shattered,
        "I trust in Thee."

I will not doubt, though all my prayers return
    Unanswered from the still, white realm above;
    I shall believe it is an all-wise Love
Which has refused those things for which I yearn;
    And though, at times, I cannot keep from grieving,
    Yet the pure ardor of my fixed believing
        Undimmed shall burn.

I will not doubt, though sorrows fall like rain,
    And troubles swarm like bees about a hive;
    I shall believe the heights for which I strive,
Are only reached by anguish and by pain;
    And, though I groan and tremble with my crosses,
    I yet shall see, through my severest losses,
        The greater gain.

I will not doubt; well anchored in the faith,
    Like some stanch ship, my soul braves every gale,
    So strong its courage that it will not fail
To breast the mighty, unknown sea of death.
    Oh, may I cry when body parts with spirit,
    "I do not doubt," so listening worlds may hear it
        With my last breath.

        Ella Wheeler Wilcox

Whatever Is--Is Best

I know, as my life grows older,
  And mine eyes have clearer sight,
That under each rank wrong somewhere
  There lies the root of Right;
That each sorrow has its purpose,
  By the sorrowing oft unguessed;
But as sure as the sun brings morning,
  Whatever is--is best.

...I know that the soul is aided
  Sometimes by the heart's unrest,
And to grow means often to suffer--
  But whatever is--is best.

I know there are no errors,
  In the great Eternal plan,
And all things work together
  For the final good of man. [humanity]
And I know when my soul speeds onward,
  In its grand Eternal quest,
I shall say as I look back earthward,
  Whatever is-- is best.

        Ella Wheeler Wilcox

114

Louisa May Alcott

(In Memoriam)

As the wind at play with a spark
  Of fire that glows through the night,
As the speed of the soaring lark
  That wings to the sky his flight,

So swiftly thy soul has sped
  On its upward, wonderful way,
Like the lark, when the dawn is red,
  In search of the shining day.

Thou art not with the frozen dead
  Whom earth in the earth we lay,
While the bearers softly tread,
  And the mourners kneel and pray;

From thy semblance, dumb and stark,
  The soul has taken its flight--
Out of the finite dark,
  Into the Infinite Light.

Louise Chandler Mounton

Soul, Wherefore Fret Thee?

*Soul, wherefore fret thee? Striving still
      to throw*
Some light upon the primal mystery
Through rolling ages pondered ceaselessly,
*Whence thou hast come, and whither thou
      shalt go!*
*Some deepest, secret voice gives thee to
      know*
How older than created earth and sea,
Thou hast been ever, shalt forever be,--
*Unborn--undying! Thy own life doth
      show,*
Yester, today, to-morrow, but a chain
*Of dusky pearls, whereof we seek in
      vain*
*End or beginning, though perchance the
      one*
*We call Today gleams whitest in the
      sun.*
Ay, Soul, thy very Self is unto thee
Immortal pledge of Immortality!

Gertrude Bloede
(Pen-name Stuart Sterne)

Death

Death that struck when I was most confiding
In my certain faith of joy to be--
Strike again, Time's withered branch dividing
From the fresh root of Eternity!

Leaves, upon Time's branch, were growing brightly,
Full sap, and full of silver dew;
Birds beneath its shelter gathered nightly;
Daily round its flowers the wild bees flew.

Sorrow passed, and plucked the golden blossom;
Guilt stripped off the foliage in its pride;
But, within its parent's kindly bosom,
Flowed for ever Life's restoring tide.

Little mourned I for the parted gladness,
For the vacant nest and silent song--
Hope was there, and laughed me out of sadness,
Whispering, "Winter will not linger long!"

And, behold! with tenfold increase blessing,
Spring adorned the beauty-burdened spray;
Wind and rain and fervent heat, caressing,
Lavished glory on that second May!

High it rose--no wing'ed grief could sweep it;
Sin was scared to distance with its shine;
Love, and its own life, had power to keep it
From all wrong--from every blight but thine!

Cruel death! The young leaves droop and languish;
Evening's gentle air may still restore--
No! the morning sunshine mocks my anguish--
Time, for me, must never blossom more!

Strike it down, that other boughs may flourish
Where that perished sapling used to be;
Thus, at least, its mouldering corpse will nourish
That from which it sprung--ETERNITY.

Emily Bronte

117

On Death

You would know the secret of death.
But how shall you find it unless you seek
it in the heart of life?
The owl whose night-bound eyes are
blind unto the day cannot unveil the mystery
of light.
If you would indeed behold the spirit of
death, open your heart wide unto the body
of life.
For life and death are one, even as the
river and the sea are one.

In the depth of your hopes and desires
lies your silent knowledge of the beyond;
And like seeds dreaming beneath the snow
your heart dreams of spring.
Trust the dreams, for in them is hidden
the gate to eternity.
Your fear of death is but the trembling
of the shepherd when he stands before the
king whose hand is to be laid upon him in
honour.
Is the shepherd not joyful beneath his
trembling, that he shall wear the mark of
the king?
Yet is he not more mindful of his trem-
bling?

For what is it to die but to stand naked
in the wind and to melt into the sun?
And what is it to cease breathing, but to
free the breath from its restless tides, that
it may rise and expand and seek God unen-
cumbered?

Only when you drink from the river of
silence shall you indeed sing.
And when you have reached the moun-
tain top, then you shall begin to climb.
And when the earth shall claim your
limbs, then you shall truly dance.

Kahlil Gibran, The Prophet, Reprinted by
permission of Alfred A. Knopf, Inc., Copyright
1923 by Kahlil Gibran and renewed 1951 by
administrators C.T.A. of Kahlil Gibran Estate
and Mary G. Gibran, pp. 80, 81.

My Hereafter

Do not come when I am dead
To sit beside a low green mound,
Or bring the first gay daffodils
Because I love them so,
For I shall not be there.
You canot find me there.

I will look up at you from the eyes
Of little children;
I will bend to meet you in the swaying boughs
Of bud-thrilled trees,
And caress you with the passionate sweep
Of storm-filled winds;
I will give you strength in your upward tread
Of everlasting hills;
I will cool your tired body in the flow
Of the limpid river;
I will warm your work-glorified hands through the glow
Of the winter fire;
I will soothe you into forgetfulness to the drop, drop
Of the rain on the roof;
I will speak to you out of the rhymes
Of the Masters;
I will dance with you in the lilt
Of the violin,
And make your heart leap with the bursting cadence
Of the organ;
I will flood your soul with the flaming radiance
Of the sunrise,
And bring you peace in the tender rose and gold
Of the after-sunset.

All these have made me happy:
They are a part of me;
I shall become a part of them.

Juanita de Long

Chapter 5

Alternative Holiday Celebrations

Introduction

Through the years, as my religious and political views diverged more and more from the norm in the United States, I grew increasingly discontent with traditional holiday rituals. I found myself flinching as I participated in rituals that endorsed values in direct violation to my own. So many holiday rituals of our culture subtly reinforced racism, sexism, classism, elitist power structures, and excessive materialism. I realized that by continuing to participate in these rituals, I was subtly reinforcing these values. Participating in rituals that were in violation to my values concerned me particularly as I thought of raising children. I began to ask myself what holiday celebrations I would want to pass on to them. My discontent led me to reexamine all of the holiday rituals that I was participating in, and to reevaluate whether each one of them was congruent with my political and religious beliefs.

In this chapter I have outlined the conclusions I arrived at regarding the major religious and political holiday rituals of our culture. For each, I've described the political and religious disagreements I had that led to my either redesigning the ritual, or to my decision to discontinue celebrating it. I also share some ideas for new holiday rituals.

I hope that by sharing the ways I have personally redesigned many of the holidays of our culture to be more in harmony with my values, I can help other people, who are experiencing similar dissatisfactions, to create holidays that are more congruent with their needs. Holiday rituals serve a very important function: they allow us time from normal, daily routines to relax, rejoice and celebrate life. They also serve as a time to examine and reflect upon our life-paths and to refocus and redirect ourselves to be more in tune with our deepest goals and values. It is therefore important that holiday rituals do indeed represent values congruent with our own so that they can truly be a time of celebration and spiritual reattunement. I hope that the information I have presented in this chapter will help those of you who are feeling alienated and disillusioned with holiday celebrations to reclaim your holidays as times of joy and inspiration. Please be aware that the ideas I have presented are meant only as suggestions to encourage readers to design their own holiday rituals unique to their needs and values.

You will notice that in many cases I designed my alternative holidays to be celebrated on the same day as the traditional holidays they were replacing. I did this for several reasons. First it makes things so much easier logistically. Adults have the day off from work and children are off from school. I also chose to design my alternative holidays this way because I discovered in my research that this strategy was a tried and true one. Many Christian holidays were deliberately set up on the same days as former pagan holidays with the belief that it would be easier for people to make the transition.

JANUARY

New Year's Eve and Day

I address New Year's Eve and Day under my discussion of Christmas.

Martin Luther King Jr.'s Birthday

I have included Martin Luther King Jr.'s birthday in my discussion of Washington's and Lincoln's birthdays below.

FEBRUARY

Abraham Lincoln's, George Washington's, and Martin Luther King Jr.'s Birthdays:

After giving these holidays considerable thought, I decided to discontinue celebrating them for several reasons. Let me begin with George Washington. One reason George Washington is "heroized" in our culture is because he was a "great general." I have been a pacifist for many years. As a result of my feelings about war, I have become uncomfortable with the idea of honoring "great generals": generals no longer seem like heros to me.

Washington is also glorified because he played a significant part in setting up the structure of our government. In certain ways, I do respect the efforts of George Washington and the other creators of our governmental structure. However, I can't help but also feel a certain amount of anger at Washington's (as well as the other founders') bigotry and sexism. Washington's concern for equality and justice did not extend to women, blacks, or Native Americans. The constitution Washington created guaranteed freedom and equality to <u>white males</u>. As a matter of fact, George Washington, being a wealthy land-owner with disdain for the poor, favored land ownership as a prerequisite for voting privileges! I do not mean to make George Washington into a terrible villain; I realize he lived in an era of unquestioned racism and sexism. However, I no longer feel comfortable paying tribute to Washington as a hero. If I were interested in picking a hero's birthday to celebrate and make a national holiday, I have to say there are thousands of people I would pick before George Washington.

However, I am not interested in picking heros and observing their birthdays as holidays. This leads me to the major reason I do not celebrate Washington's, Lincoln's or Martin Luther King Jr.'s birthdays. I do not celebrate any of these men's birthdays as holidays because I no longer support the idea of heroization. Through the years, I have become more and more aware of the absurdity of singling out particular people and bestowing upon them the credit and glory for accomplishments that are, in fact, the result of the total efforts of humanity--built from hour to hour, year to year, and century to century. Heroization ignores the contributions of 99.9% of the people!

To return to George Washington, as an example of this point, Washington is heroized as the founding father of the "egalitarian", "democratic" governmental structure of this country. However, the contributions that Washington made toward "equality and justice for all" were just one minute part of the overall process of establishing equality in this country--a struggle that continues today.

The fact that we in this society are taught to narrowly focus our admiration, and idolize a few people and ignore all others becomes obvious if you examine an "alternative" calendar, i.e., one that commemorates women, blacks, social activists, etc. On these calendars, each day commemorates people who have made contributions through the centuries toward goals such as peace, democracy, racial equality, women's equality etc.

Looking at such a calendar, one begins to see the absurdity of singling out Washington or Lincoln or even "counterculture" heros like Malcolm X, or Martin Luther King Jr. It quickly becomes obvious that there are countless heros and heroines who have made invaluable contributions to the welfare of humanity. Here are a few examples from alternative calendars to demonstrate my point:

January 21: Margaret Brent becomes the first American woman to claim the right to vote--1647.

February 2: Anthony Benezet refuses to pay taxes during the Revolutionary War, becoming one of the earliest resistors of United States war taxes--1779.

May 1: First general strike called to demonstrate for the eight-hour day for all American workers--1886.

June 27: Emma Goldman, feminist, avowed anarchist, radical labor organizer, and writer born--1869.

September 1: Gabriel Prusser, Virginia slave, leads mass revolt--1800.

November 20: A landing party of seventy-eight Indians calling themselves "Indians of All Tribes" occupy Alcatraz Island in San Francisco Bay demanding that the land be returned to the Indians. This event gives new life to the Native American Rights Movement--1969.

In summary, I do not celebrate Washington's, Lincoln's or Martin Luther King's birthdays because they are just three people of millions who have struggled for equality in this country. To make a national holiday of every person's birthday who has contributed to the welfare of humanity would be impossible. Therefore, I have tried to design alternative holidays that have as their focus a given ideal, as opposed to focusing on one particular hero/heroine who worked towards that ideal. Thus, as an alternative holiday to Washington's, Lincoln's, or Martin Luther King Jr.'s birthdays, I designed a holiday that I called World Equality Day.

Alternative Holiday: World Equality Day

See description under month of July.

Valentine's Day

In order to evaluate whether I wanted to continue celebrating Valentine's Day, I had to research the historical origins of the holiday since I was unfamiliar with how and why Saint Valentine's Day came into being. I discovered that Valentine's Day was one of several holidays practiced long before there were reliable written records. Thus the meaning and significance of the holiday are somewhat difficult to determine. After consulting several source books on the subject, I found it impossible to determine which of the various explanations was the correct one. I suspect there is some truth and some distortion in each of them. I have listed below the most accepted explanations for the holiday's origin.

1) Saint Valentine is believed to have been a priest under Roman Emperor Claudius. The emperor was having difficulty getting soldiers to go to war because they did not want to leave their wives. The emperor therefore outlawed all marriages and engagements. Valentine defied the emperor's decree and secretly married couples. He was caught and jailed, and died in prison. Thus, Valentine emerged as the patron saint of lovers.

2) Another version is that Saint Valentine was imprisoned for helping Christians. While in prison, he and the jailor's daughter fell in love and exchanged love letters, which he signed "Your Valentine." Thus, Saint Valentine was linked to the idea of passionate, romantic love transcending all political, religious, and practical considerations.

3) It is a longheld belief in Europe that February 14th is the time when birds choose their mates. Thus, the custom arose of people choosing their spouses on February 14th.

4) There was a Roman feast called Lupercalia which was celebrated on February 14th. During this feast, all the young women's names were put into a box and drawn by the young men. The couples would then be partners for the festivals, and the young man was supposed to act as a suitor to the young lady for the remainder of the year. This custom was very popular for several centuries. As Christianity took root, this custom was discouraged. The church forbade the practice and instead put the names of saints in the boxes. The young man would then draw the name of a saint and he was then supposed to try to emulate that saint in the coming year.

Having familiarized myself with the historical origins of Valentine's Day, I concluded that it seemed to have rather admirable or at least harmless origins. There was no political or religious meaning attached to the holiday that I found offensive. I consider romantic, passionate love to be one of the greatest joys of my life, so I decided to continue celebrating this holiday.

However, I do have a lot of disagreements with the way the holiday is commonly practiced in the United States today. Like many holidays in this country, Valentine's Day has become heavily commercialized. Spend, spend, spend has become the major focus of the holiday. There seems to be no limit to the number of red trinkets, clothes, etc., that one is encouraged to buy for one's "valentine" lest they not feel loved. The idea of receiving red lace negligees and having my lover spend a hundred dollars on a fancy dinner has never appealed to me.

I have always celebrated Valentine's Day by exchanging small presents, perhaps a book or record, and cooking a nice dinner with my partner at home. At times when I've had no lover, I have always tried to get together with another single friend for dinner so I didn't sit around and get depressed because "nobody loved me."

Reconsidering this holiday during the process of writing this book prompted me to come up with some ideas to improve my celebration of this holiday. I began thinking about the fact that it takes a lot more than romantic dinners and nice presents to keep passionate, romantic love alive and well. I thought what a good idea it would be to include some personal growth or self-awareness exercises as part of the holiday ritual. Valentine's Day could be a time for lovers to really talk about their relationship, a time to talk about steps they could take in the coming year to nurture their love. Examples of some exercises are listed below:

1) Share qualities you really like about each other.

2) Share three fears you have about your relationship and ideas for dealing with those fears.

3) Write down and post five fun activities you would like to do together in the coming year.

4) Give one another five helpful hints about what each of you can do in the future to nurture the passionate, romantic aspect of your relationship. These can be affirmations of things the other person is doing that you like, or suggestions for some things you would like from them:

Examples:

I feel really close and affectionate toward you when you call me from work and tell me you miss me.

I feel really sexually turned on when you kiss me really intensely before initiating intercourse.

Let's set aside one night, every two weeks, where we stay home and don't answer the phone or work around the house, and let's give each other our undivided attention.

Let's take a massage class together.

The possibilities for these types of exercises are endless. Another way my partner and I have started celebrating Valentine's Day is that we each pick a reading from a book, article, or poem dealing with how to create and maintain a successful love relationship, and read them to one another. The following example is one that I have read to my partner:

A good relationship has a pattern like a dance and is built on some of the same rules. The partners do not need to hold on tightly, because they move confidently in the same pattern, intricate but gay and swift and free, like a country dance of Mozart's. To touch heavily would be to arrest the pattern and freeze the movement, to check the endlessly changing beauty of its unfolding. There is no place here for the possessive clutch, the clinging arm, the heavy hand; only the barest touch in passing. Now arm in arm, now face to face, now back to back--it does not matter which. Because they know they are partners moving to the same rhythm, creating a pattern together, and being invisibly nourished by it. . . .The dancers who are perfectly in time never destroy "the winged life" in each other or in themselves.
. . . The "veritable life" of our emotions and our relationship also is intermittent. When you love someone you do not love them all the time, in exactly the same way, from moment to moment. It is an impossibility. It is even a lie to pretend to. And yet this is exactly what most of us demand. We have so little faith in the ebb and flow of life, of love, of

relationships. We leap at the flow of the tide and resist in terror its ebb. We are afraid it will never return. We insist on permanency, on duration, on continuity; when the only continuity possible, in life as in love, is in growth, in fluidity--in freedom, in the sense that the dancers are free, barely touching as they pass, but partners in the same pattern. The only real security is not in owning or possessing, not in demanding or expecting, not in hoping, even. Security in a relationship lies neither in looking back to what it was in nostalgia, nor forward to what it might be in dread or anticipation, but living in the present relationship and accepting it as it is now. For relationships, too, must be like islands. One must accept them for what they are here and now, within their limits--islands, surrounded and interrupted by the sea, continually visited and abandoned by the tides. One must accept the security of the winged life, of ebb and flow, of intermittency.

. . . Perhaps this is the most important thing for me to take back from beach-living; simply the memory that each cycle of the tide is valid; each cycle of the wave is valid; each cycle of a relationship is valid.

Anne Morrow Lindbergh, Gift from the Sea, 1955, Reprinted with permission from Random House Inc., New York, pp. 104, 105, 108, 109, 110.

I hope you find these suggestions for ways to celebrate Valentine's Day helpful. Many of these ideas would also be applicable for anniversary celebrations.

MARCH

Easter/Good Friday

I, like most everyone in our Christianity-dominated culture, was quite familiar with the origins of Easter as a holiday, and I celebrated it as a major holiday. However, as my beliefs began diverging from the teachings of Christianity, I became more and more uncomfortable with the idea of celebrating Easter.

The entire basis of the holiday Easter is the commemoration of the resurrection of Jesus as the long-awaited Christ. As I have outlined previously, I do not believe in Jesus as "the Christ," the divine messenger from God the Father. (I don't, in fact, believe in the concept of christs or in God the Father. See chapter 1.) I believe the story of Jesus's resurrection to be a myth. I think that many of the myths that have been passed down to us about Jesus, particularly his resurrection, evolved because he was a enigma to the people of his time. I think that many of Jesus's ideas, e.g., "love thine enemy" were so revolutionary and ahead of his time, that the people he preached to found him quite difficult to comprehend. Defining Jesus as a christ was the only way people could make sense out of who he was.

Realizing that I no longer believed in the Christian basis of Easter, I decided that it made no sense for me to continue celebrating it. I therefore decided to design an alternative spring holiday. In order to design my spring holiday, I decided to research ancient spring holidays to generate some ideas. I was surprised to discover that Easter was originally a pagan holiday, named for the Saxon goddess Eostre. Easter was celebrated the first Sunday after the first full moon after the spring equinox. It was believed that the goddess Eostre passed into her fertile season at this time. Easter eggs were symbols of fertility. Even the Easter bunny was a pagan concept--originally the sacred hare of the goddess.

It appears to me that both the Christian myths of the re-birth of Jesus as well as the goddess-centered myths surrounding the Goddess Eostre were attempts to express the rejuvenation and re-birth of nature that is so overwhelmingly apparent each spring. I, too, felt a need for some kind of spring holiday, however, I wanted the holiday to be free of archaic religious myths with which I disagreed. Therefore, as an alternative holiday to Easter, I began celebrating the Spring Equinox.

Alternative Holiday: Spring Equinox

Celebrating the solstices and equinoxes is becoming quite common in places where the so-called "counter-culture" flourishes. Thus, in Ann Arbor, one is often wished "Happy Spring Equinox" in place of "Happy Easter" or greeted in December with "Happy Solstice" in place of "Merry Christmas." I have found the earth's seasonal cycles to be an excellent basis for holiday celebrations.

For several years I have celebrated the solstices and equinoxes by getting together with friends for pot-luck dinners. We celebrate by reading poems and by doing group meditation together. The following poem, which I wrote and read at a spring equinox celebration several years ago, will, I think, give you a sense of the meaning of the holiday.

A Poem For A Spring Equinox Celebration

Today we come together to
rejoice in the reawakening of the earth.
We again witness the Divine harmony of the seasons of our planet.
We are filled with a sense of wonderment
and awe,
As we witness this miraculous rebirth of life.

Let us, like the earth,
reawaken to the joy and wonder of our lives.
Let us call forth now, the seeds
we have long nurtured within ourselves.
May the warm sunshine help us to bring our
dreams and aspirations to fruition.

As the earth in the spring provides for the needs
of all living beings,
By giving warm rains and sunshine,
that all will be nurtured and grow,
Let us remember to provide each other with what we
need to blossom and grow:
Love, support, encouragement, forgiveness and
patience.

We will take this time to express through song and
dance,
Our love for our beautiful planet,
And our joy in existence.

I try to include both serious and fun activities in my solstice/equinox celebrations. Thus, besides meditation and poetry, my friends and I celebrate the spring equinox with dancing. Dancing is an excellent means of celebrating holidays. Yet in our culture no dancing of any kind is included in our holiday celebrations. The type of dancing I have found most suited for holiday celebrations is square dancing. Square dancing is perfect for community holiday celebrations because it is very joyous and uplifting, it can be done by people of all ages, and it fosters a tremendous sense of community. In addition, square dancing satisfies a very important human need: touching. Square dancing provides the opportunity for lots of touching; men with men, women with women, as well as women with men.

My friends and I have included going to community square dances as part of our holiday celebrations for many years now. Every spring there is an all-night square dance in Ann Arbor, complete with childcare. If holiday square dancing sounds appealing to you, find out if there are any square dances held in your community. If not, you can organize one. You can hire a folk music group, complete with a square dance caller and teacher, for a few hundred dollars. Rent a school gymnasium or small hall and charge participants a small admission fee to cover costs. (Three to four dollars is average for square dance admission.) I think you will find many eager square dancers out there!

MAY

Memorial Day

I made a decision to stop celebrating Memorial Day because I believe it to be a war-affirming holiday: I have always thought that the grieving that is done on Memorial Day for all the American soldiers who lost their lives in wars throughout the centuries is intertwined with glorifying war. I believe that grieving for American soldiers has far too narrow a focus: we need to broaden our focus to grieve for all of the soldiers' lives lost, on all sides, in all wars. Furthermore, I think it is imperative that while grieving for all the soldiers' lives lost, we challenge the morality of war itself.

> *An alternative Memorial Day celebration will recall not only the tragedy of lives lost, but will also confess the futility of war itself as a means to resolve conflict.*
>
> Milo Thornberry, *The Alternative Celebrations Catalog*, 1982, The Pilgrim Press, New York, p. 66.

I was interested in developing a holiday to replace Memorial Day that would have a strong anti-war orientation and a global rather than national focus. Therefore, as an alternative to Memorial Day, I designed a holiday which I call World Peace Day.

Alternative Holiday: World Peace Day

There are many organizations that define various days as peace holidays. I chose to celebrate my peace day in May in place of Memorial Day, because it fits with my goal of slowly eliminating holidays that I believe are ill-suited to the needs of today, by transforming them into new holidays. I define World Peace Day as a

127

time to try to further develop within myself a consciousness of peace. I devote time and energy to making some small personal contribution toward a more peaceful world. World peace must start within each person as Marilyn Ferguson put it so beautifully:

> . . .Peace is a state of mind, not a state of the nation. Without personal transformation, the people of the world will be forever locked in conflict.
>
> If we limit ourselves to the old-paradigm concept of averting war, we are trying to overpower darkness rather than switching on the light. If we reframe the problem--if we think of fostering community, health, innovation, self-discovery, purpose--we are already engaged in waging peace. In a rich, creative, meaningful environment there is no room for hostility.
>
> War is unthinkable in a society of autonomous people who have discovered the connectedness of all humanity, who are unafraid of alien ideas and alien cultures, who know that all revolutions begin within and that you cannot impose your brand of enlightenment on anyone else.
>
> . . .We need not wait for a leadership. We can begin to effect change at any point in a complex system: a human life, a family, a nation. One person can create a transformative environment for others through trust and friendship. A warm family or community can make a stranger feel at ease. A society can encourage growth and renewal in its members.
>
> We can begin anywhere--everywhere. "Let there be peace," says a bumper sticker, "and let it begin with me." Let there be health, learning, relationship, right uses of power, meaningful work. . . .Let there be transformation, and let it begin with me.

Marilyn Ferguson, *The Aquarian Conspiracy*, Copyright 1980 by Marilyn Ferguson. Reprinted by permission of the publisher, Jeremy P. Tarcher, Inc., Los Angeles, pp. 411-12.

If the idea of World Peace Day sounds appealing to you, I offer the following suggestions as possible ways to observe the holiday:

1) Write a letter to your congress-person, newspapers, etc. requesting support of peace-oriented legislation.

2) Do some volunteer work for one of the many organizations involved in peace work.

3) Make a financial contribution to a peace activist organization.

4) Organize or participate in a war protest demonstration.

5) There are often a number of peace protesters in jail. Writing supportive letters to political prisoners can help make their prison time much easier.

6) Organize a moment of silence to grieve for the loss of soldiers' lives, on all sides, in all wars through a local radio station. Follow the moment of silence with poetry or a reading that challenges war as an

institution.

7) Rent a video cassette recorder and show a movie to family, friends, or general members of the community that has an anti-war message. Some examples of movies you might consider showing are "War Games", "Ghandi", "Platoon", "Apocalypse Now", "All Quiet On The Western Front", "King of Hearts", "Johnnie Got His Gun", "Coming Home." You might want to rent a room in a school or library and advertise that you will be showing peace-oriented movies from noon till midnight.

The following are some more personal methods of working toward world peace:

1) Read an inspirational book that helps you reaffirm the possibility of world peace and gives you ideas about what individuals can do to help create a peaceful world.

2) One exercise that I tried and found extremely helpful was not allowing myself to use any violent language for a week. E.g. no "He's such an asshole," no "I hate. . ." etc. If you try this exercise, you may discover as I did, that you carry quite a lot of negative energy within you. Believing in peace, and living a life of peace, are totally different things, I discovered!

3) Another experience I found helpful is to invite a group of friends over and engage in some conflict resolution games. (You could also do this within your own family.) You can get books that contain many Values Dilemma exercises, e.g. "Who do you throw off the sinking life-raft?" As a group using consensus decision-making (everyone must agree), come to a group decision about what to do in the simulated situation. These types of exercises are extremely helpful in developing the skills necessary for world peace: acceptance of others' values, consideration of others' needs, ability to be flexible and to compromise, creativity, and so on.

4) Another idea for World Peace Day is to make peace with anyone with whom you have a conflict. Allow yourself to let go of the pent-up hostility that you feel toward that person. Let yourself see the God that lies within that individual, despite whatever characteristics he/she may have that you do not like. You may not ever be able to like this person, but can you learn to accept him/her?

There are endless possibilities: any activity that helps foster world peace. I'm sure you can develop many creative ways to observe this holiday.

JUNE

Summer Solstice

As I mentioned earlier, many people have begun celebrating the cycles of the earth. My friends and I celebrate the solstices and equinoxes by coming together for a pot-luck dinner. We read poems together and sing songs. I have included a poem that I wrote and read at one of our summer solstice celebrations below. I think it captures the essence of the holiday.

Summer Solstice Poem

We come together today to give thanks for this
beautiful planet that ever provides its bounty for our
sustenance.

The rigorous spring planting is over.
We have witnessed the seeds reawaken, as the earth
pours forth its endless strength and vitality.
We joyously behold the wondrous splendor of summer.

Today we renew our appreciation and wonder
for the Divine balance and harmony of the earth,
   And we reaffirm our commitment to live in
reverence of nature.

As we watch the earth so jubilantly and lovingly
nurture our crops,
   May we also be inspired to give from our
hearts.
   As we watch the earth pour forth its gifts to us,
May we feel called upon to give of ourselves more fully
in whatever work we are engaged.

As we witness the harmonious cycles of the earth,
may our faith in a loving universe be renewed.

Another activity my friends and I have begun to include in our holiday celebrations is playing games together. You may be familiar with what are known as "New Games," popularized in books like The New Games Book by Andrew Fluegelman and the New Games Foundation and The Cooperative Sports and Games Book by Terry Orlick. The creators of New Games define them as follows:

Games are not so much a way to compare our abilities as a way to
celebrate them. . . .By reexamining the basic idea of play, we could
involve families, groups, and individuals in a joyous recreation experience
that creates a sense of community and personal expression. People could
center on the joy of playing, cooperating, and trusting, rather than
striving to win.

Andrew Fluegelman and The New Games Foundation, The New Games
Book, Tiburon, Calif., Headlands Press, 1976, p. 10.

I strongly encourage you to read these books and urge you to consider incorporating noncompetitive, community games into your holiday celebrations. These books offer games for as few as two people and as many as several hundred. I think your family and friends will find it quite exhilarating to discover that six-year-olds and sixty-year-olds can play together and all have a great time!

JULY

Fourth of July/Independence Day

After contemplating the meaning and origins of the Fourth of July, I concluded that I was uncomfortable celebrating this holiday because of its nationalistic orientation. I decided it was too much of a tragic irony to celebrate that we in the United States are free of colonial rule and taxation, when we have become one of the most powerful and oppressive colonizers in the world today. As I thought about the gruesome practices the U.S. government perpetrates upon the people of Third World countries in order to rape them of resources, I found myself unable to find any joy in celebrating our freedom from colonization by England.

I concluded that holidays such as the Fourth of July, which has such a strong patriotic focus, hinder the development of a global-citizen consciousness, which I think is essential for the survival of the human race on this planet. I thus decided I wanted to design an alternative holiday that would have as its focus freedom from oppression and exploitation for all peoples of the world. Therefore, in lieu of the Fourth of July, I created a holiday which I coined World Equality Day.

Alternative Holiday: World Equality Day

I define World Equality Day as a time to promote a more egalitarian world. There are a variety of holidays designated by various groups which deal with the issue of equality: Women's Equality Day (anniversary of women's attainment of suffrage), Black Awareness Week, Week of Solidarity with the Peoples Struggling Against Racism and Racial Discrimination, National Freedom Day, May Day, Race Unity Day, and on and on. However, I decided to celebrate World Equality Day on the same day as the Fourth of July because, as I discussed earlier, I am trying to design alternative holidays that can be celebrated in place of traditional holidays. If you like the idea of World Equality Day, I hope you will find the following suggestions for ways to observe the holiday helpful.

1) An excellent way to observe World Equality Day is to engage in activities that foster what I call an "equality consciousness." For instance, participating in Values Clarification exercises that require a group to come to a decision using consensus decision-making, where all group members have equal voting rights, can help develop the skills necessary to create an egalitarian society. Equality is a noble concept, but in order for it to come about, people must learn how to manifest egalitarian ways of interacting in their everyday lives.

2) There are also a variety of games available that help foster "equality consciousness." The games are simulations of the energy, resources, and population of the earth. The object of the games is to manipulate the earth's energy and resources so as to adequately provide shelter, food, and other life necessities for the entire global population. Playing games such as these with your family or friends would be a good way to participate in World Equality Day.

3) A logical way to observe World Equality Day is to do some volunteer work for an organization dealing with equality issues, whether

it be for blacks, Native Americans, women, or Third World peoples. Unfortunately, there is an almost endless list of oppressed groups.

4) Something we have started to do as a family to observe World Equality Day is to read a poem, article, etc. at the evening meal which deals with the issue of equality. I am including one of my favorites below. I think it captures the idea that to create an egalitarian society, we as individuals must live a personal lifestyle which promotes a consciousness of equality:

The Shakertown Pledge

Recognizing that the earth and the fulness thereof is a gift from our gracious God, and that we are called to cherish, nurture, and provide loving stewardship for the earth's resources,

And recognizing that life itself is a gift, and a call to responsibility, joy, and celebration, I make the following declarations:

1. I declare myself to be a world citizen.

2. I commit myself to lead an ecologically sound life.

3. I commit myself to lead a life of creative simplicity and to share my personal wealth with the world's poor.

4. I commit myself to join with others in the reshaping of institutions in order to bring about a more just global society in which all people have full access to the needed resources for their physical, emotional, intellectual, and spiritual growth.

5. I commit myself to occupational accountability, and so doing I will seek to avoid the creation of products which cause harm to others.

6. I affirm the gift of my body and commit myself to its proper nourishment and physical well-being.

7. I commit myself to examine continually my relations with others, and to attempt to relate honestly, morally, and lovingly to those around me.

8. I commit myself to personal renewal through prayer, meditation, and study.

9. I commit myself to responsible participation in a

community of faith.

Adam Daniel Finnerty, <u>No More Plastic Jesus</u>, Mary-Knoll, New York, Orbis Books, 1977, p. 97. Reprinted with permission.

If you like the concept of World Equality Day, I'm sure you will come up with many creative ways to observe the holiday.

SEPTEMBER

Labor Day

In order to evaluate whether I wanted to change the way I celebrated Labor Day, I had to do quite a lot of research about the origins of the holiday. Therefore, the background information I have included about Labor Day is somewhat lengthy. However, I felt that in order for readers to evaluate whether they wanted to redesign their Labor Day celebrations, it was necessary to present them with an adequate history of the political origins of the holiday.

The first time a day was designated as a labor holiday was in the early 1800's. The Central Labor Union of New York passed a resolution in 1882 that the fifth of September be proclaimed a general holiday for the workingmen and proposed "that parades and other festivities take place." The Central Labor Union also urged other unions throughout the country to celebrate September 5th as a universal holiday for workingmen.

In 1884, the Federation of Organized Trade and Labor Unions of the U.S. and Canada (soon to become the American Federation of Labor) carried the Central Labor Union's idea of a labor day a step further. They made the following resolution:

> *Resolved, that the first Monday in September of each year be set aside as Laborers' national holiday, and that we recommend its observance by all wage workers, irrespective of sex, calling, or nationality.*

> *Convention Proceedings, Federation of Organized Trades, 1884, p. 23, cited in Phillip Foner, <u>History of the Labor Movement in the United States</u>, International Publishers, New York, 1955, p. 97.*

The concept of Labor Day was enthusiastically received throughout the country. There were massive parades, speeches, political rallies, and marches in cities across the nation.

During the same years that the first Monday of September was initiated as a holiday to honor laborers, American labor unions were unwittingly planting the seeds for a labor holiday whose scope and significance would surpass the labor day celebrated the first Monday of September: May Day.

In 1884, the Federation of Organized Trade and Labor Unions of the U.S. and Canada, which had been active in establishing Labor Day as a holiday, began massive organizing for the eight-hour day for all U.S. workers. They passed the following resolution:

> *. . .Resolved that eight hours shall constitute a legal day's labor   from*

and after May 1, 1886, and that we recommend to labor organizations
throughout this district that they so direct their laws as to conform to this
resolution by the time named.

Proceedings, Federation of Trade and Labor Unions, 1884, pp. 10-14, 24-25,
cited in Phillip Foner, May Day: A Short History 1886--1986, International
Publishers, New York, 1986.

On May 1, 1886, there were massive strikes and work stoppages in cities throughout the United States. Estimates of the number of strikers ran as high as half a million. The entire city of Chicago was brought to a standstill.

Unfortunately, the worker strikes for the eight-hour day on May 1, 1886 were followed by a tragedy. During a rally at Haymarket Square in Chicago, to protest the police brutality that had been used against the striking workers, a bomb exploded in the crowd, killing one policeman and wounding seventy.

Eight anarchist/socialists, militant organizers for the eight-hour day strikes, were selected to stand trial as a result of the Haymarket bomb incident. Only one of these eight men was present at Haymarket Square, and he was speaking at the time of the incident and not in a position to have thrown the bomb. However, the eight were indicted for murder of the policeman killed at Haymarket. They were not indicted for throwing the bomb, but were accused of the murder on the grounds that their past speeches and "propaganda" had influenced the anonymous person who threw the bomb! The eight were collectively charged and convicted of conspiracy to commit murder.

The case received international attention. Letters poured in from all over the world asking that the eight men not be executed. The indictment of these men was seen the world over as a tragic injustice. It was obvious they were being persecuted because of their political views and because of their work in organizing workers. The state attorney general's summation speech to the jury openly admitted as much:

Law is on trial. Anarchy is on trial. These men have been selected,
picked out by the grand jury, and indicted because they were leaders. They
are no more guilty than the thousands who follow them. Gentlemen of the
jury; convict these men, make examples of them, hang them and save our
institutions, our society.

Henry David, The History of the Haymarket Affair, New York, 1936, pp.
234-54, 297-300, cited in Foner, May Day.

Three of the eight accused were hung, one committed suicide or was murdered in his cell, and the others were sentenced to life imprisonment.

Spurred by the success of the May 1st workers' strikes, and fueled by the unjust hanging of the men who are known today as the Haymarket Martyrs, May 1st soon developed into a labor holiday.

In December of 1888, the American Federation of Labor (A.F.L.) proclaimed that May 1, 1890, was the day that organized labor would enforce the eight-hour day, via a mass strike if necessary. In 1889, the Second Socialist International (an international congress of Socialist delegates from various countries), in support of the A.F.L.'s plan to rally for the eight-hour day, passed the following resolution:

A great international demonstration shall be organized for a fixed date
in such a manner that the workers in all countries and in all cities shall on a
specified day simultaneously address to the public authorities a demand to fix

the workday at eight hours and to put into effect the other resolutions of the International Congress of Paris.

In view of the fact that such a demonstration has already been resolved upon by the American Federation of Labor at its convention of December 1888 in St. Louis, for May 1, 1890, that day is accepted as the day for international demonstration.

The workers of the various nations shall organize the demonstration in a manner suited to the conditions in their country.

On May 1, 1890, there were work stoppages and demonstrations throughout the world, and May Day--International Workers Day--was born:

The workers allowed nothing to hinder them from celebrating the 1st of May--not outbursts of fury from the entire bourgeois press of all countries, nor the decrees of governments, not the threats of dismissal, nor huge military levels. They celebrated everywhere; such an international celebration as the world has not yet experienced; the whole civilized world was one great May-field where millions and millions of proletarians assembled in order to draw together the demands they find essential for the further development of society.

Herbert Steiner, "The First May Day in Austria," Paper delivered at conference on the First May Day Throughout the World, Second Congress of the World Association of Institutes for the Study of the History of the Labor Movement, Mexico, 1980, pp. 1-2, cited in Foner, May Day.

American labor unions enthusiastically participated in May Day for several years. However, in the early 1900's, the large American labor unions began undergoing a conservative swing. Up until 1900, American labor unions had many socialist members and sympathies; many of the constitutions and platforms of the early unions were socialist in orientation. However, by 1900, the large American unions were becoming anti-socialist and anti-communist. Socialists began forming unions of their own like The Industrial Workers of the World (I.W.W.), which professed more radical philosophies. As the rift widened between the large American unions and the Socialists, the unions disowned May Day as a holiday because they felt it was too linked to socialism:

The struggle against Socialists inside the A.F.L. made the radical and international aspects of May Day seem a liability to conservative unionists. Soon the leadership of the A.F.L. disowned May Day as a workers' holiday, claiming that it belonged to Europe and the Socialists rather than to the United States and U.S. trade unions. They ceased to mention the origin of May Day in the United States and threw all of their support behind Labor Day. To be sure, individual unions affiliated with the A.F.L., especially those with Socialist leadership and membership, continued to participate in May Day parades and meetings. But by 1905, the A.F.L. made no references in its official publications to the Federation's role in founding May Day as a day of labor demonstration, or to the fact that May Day had originated in the United States. So far as the A.F.L. was officially concerned only Labor Day was a day to be celebrated by workers in the United States.

Foner, May Day pp. 76-77.

Despite the fact that the A. F. L. disowned May Day as a holiday, May Day continued to be celebrated in this country, though it was never to attain the scope and popularity that it received in the first ten years of its existence.

During the McCarthy era in the 1950's, there were attempts to repress May Day parades and demonstrations in this country. Permits for parades were repeatedly denied, and organizers of May Day activities were harassed for their anti-government, pro-communist beliefs. However, demonstrations were still held with marchers carrying banners such as "Freedom to the Rosenbergs", and "Resistance to McCarthyism."

Attempts were also made in the 1950's to eradicate May Day observances in this country by designating other holidays on May 1st. In 1955, May 1st was proclaimed by President Eisenhower to be Loyalty Day. Following the inception of Loyalty Day, Loyalty Day groups were given permits to hold parades, though May Day organizers were denied parade permits. In 1961, May 1st was proclaimed by President Kennedy to be Law Day. The organizers of these holidays, e.g., the Veterans of Foreign Wars, openly proclaimed that they were deliberately designing holidays on May 1st to discourage the observation of "communist" May Day.

Despite efforts by conservative groups to eradicate the celebration of May Day in the United States, liberal and radical groups continued to observe May Day. Though the observance of May Day declined in the United States during the decades from 1910-1980, the converse was true in other countries. Millions of workers from all corners of the globe rallied behind the revolutionary idea of a holiday that promoted solidarity among workers in all countries. May Day demonstrations and observances occurred in diverse countries such as Russia, England, Germany, Mexico, Costa Rica, Canada, Ireland, China, Cuba, France, Spain, Italy, Japan, Poland, South Africa, Vietnam, and Turkey.

The year 1986 marked the hundredth-year anniversary of May Day, and various political groups made a concerted effort to encourage American workers to join the rest of the world in observing May Day as an international workers' holiday:

> *May Day, born in the U.S.A. thirty-one years before the October Revolution in the U.S.S.R., is presented as though it had been secretly hatched in the Kremlin. It is portrayed as something alien to the struggles of the working class that gave it its birth. Surely it is time, and past time, for the working people of our country to reclaim their significant May Day heritage.*
>
> *Let May 1, 1986, mark the rebirth of the observance of May Day in cities across our country--across the land, whose labor movement created this mighty holiday and gave it to the workers of the world.*
>
> *Will Parry, Labor Today, May, 1985, cited in Foner, May Day, p. 159.*

Labor Day, that is, the first Monday in September, evolved along very different lines than did May Day. Labor Day initially, had a militant political orientation, similar to May Day, as the following Labor Day resolution of the Minneapolis Trades and Labor Assembly of 1884 reflected:

> *To capitalists, bankers and their hirelings, the power you possess when you thoroughly understand how to think and legislate for yourselves. While you drudge and toil away your lives for a bare existence, these idlers and non-producers live in luxury and debauchery, squandering with a lavish hand that which belongs to you--that which your labor produces.*
> *. . . They have tried to deny us the right to organize--a right guaranteed*

by the constitution of this government. Therefore we call on you to show that we defy them; that you will organize; that you have organized; that the day of your deliverance is approaching. To do this we ask you to join in our ranks in celebrating this day.

The Trades and Labor Assembly proclaims to be labor's annual holiday the first Monday of September. Leave your benches, leave your shops. . . .

St. Paul Globe Democrat, July 19, August 16, 1885, cited in Foner, History of the Labor Movement in the United States, Volume 2, p. 97.

During the first decades of Labor Day observances, there were Labor Day parades as well as speeches and rallies aimed at improving the working conditions and wages of laborers. However, as the plight of the majority of workers in this country improved, and the unions won more and more rights and benefits for their workers, Labor Day celebrations in the United States lost much of their political and social activist orientation.

Through the years, the holiday took on a more recreational focus. Additional activities such as fireworks, barbecues, state and county fairs, beauty pageants, community games, square dances, and concerts, among other activities, were added to Labor Day celebrations. Eventually Labor Day celebrations became family oriented instead of community oriented. The most common way that evolved for celebrating Labor Day was for families to escape to the state parks for a last picnic or camping trip of the summer season. This is the way most Americans still observe Labor Day in the United States in the 1980's.

After researching the origins of Labor Day I began the task of evaluating the ways I celebrated the holiday, and of considering whether I wanted to make any changes in the way I observed Labor Day.

Having grown up in a generation that was too late to witness the active years of the labor movement in this country, I had never participated in any Labor Day activities that had any political focus. For me Labor Day had always been a recreational holiday for swimming, camping, and picnicking. I hadn't even been aware of the existence of May Day until I began research for this chapter.

As I became aware of the political significance of Labor Day, I began to feel uncomfortable that the day had been transformed into a purely recreational holiday. I realized that my generation has come to take for granted the many rights and benefits that workers through the decades painfully struggled to achieve: minimum wage guarantees, child protection laws, safe working conditions, paid vacation and holidays, pensions, health insurance, and, most importantly, the right of workers to organize, strike, boycott, picket, and collectively bargain to improve their wages and working conditions. We have lost touch with the memories of how workers in this country worked fifteen-hour days for pitiful wages and were persecuted and jailed for trying to improve their condition through organizing.

The more I learned about the origins of Labor Day, the more it seemed to me that observing this holiday with nothing other than picnics and barbecues was a great dishonor to the countless workers who, through the centuries, painfully struggled to overcome their exploitation.

I also began to see that letting Labor Day become a recreational holiday, because the majority of workers in the United States had attained a comfortable middle-class existence, was a tragic oversight of the many millions of workers who are still exploited. There are still many oppressed laborers in this country: migrant farm workers, coal and copper miners, women, blacks, and scores of unemployed people! I began to realize that when we--as workers who are lucky enough to now have decent wages and rights as workers--ignore the plight of workers who are still exploited, we are violating the basic principles on which the labor movement of this country was founded: that laborers must unite <u>in solidarity</u> to work against their <u>common</u> problems until <u>all</u> workers have been rescued from exploitation.

I also became uncomfortable with the fact that May Day had been disavowed as a holiday in the United States. Because we in America do not participate in International Workers Day, we are cut off from the struggles of workers in other parts of the world. This is particularly sad because it is quite often American capitalists who are exploiting Third World workers! In many Third World countries, U.S. agribusiness conglomerates force indigent peoples off their lands and force them to become laborers on cash crop plantations. The wages and working conditions on these plantations are some of the worst in the world. On a similar note, American capitalists often move their industries overseas (where workers do not have strong labor unions to defend their rights) to avoid paying union wages and benefits to American workers.

In summary, after studying the history of Labor Day, I came to the conclusion that it was time for me, as an American worker with decent wages and benefits, to stop using Labor Day as a time to rejoice in my own good fortune and rejoin the struggles of less fortunate workers throughout the world to escape from their oppression. The next step was figuring out <u>how</u> to go about such a task.

After doing some brainstorming and talking with various people, I came up with the following ways to celebrate Labor Day, which I hope will do justice to the holiday. If, upon reading this chapter you similarly find yourself wanting to make your Labor Day celebrations have more of a political/social activist orientation, I offer the following suggestions for observing Labor Day, either in September or May:

1) Rent a room and show movies depicting the struggles of laborers past and present. Some good examples would be <u>Norma Rae</u>, <u>Reds</u>, <u>El Norte</u>, <u>The Wobblies</u>, <u>Day without Sunshine</u>, <u>Grapes of Wrath</u>, <u>The Wrath of Grapes</u>, <u>Harvest of Shame</u>. Contact labor organizations in your area for further ideas.

2) Organize a community sing-along. There are a variety of labor song-books. Some of the more popular are:

Alan Lomax, Woodie Guthrie, Pete Seger, <u>Hard Hitting Songs For Hard Hit People; American Folk Songs of the Depression and the Labor Movement of the 1930's</u>, Oak Publications, 1967.

Pete Seger and Rob Reiser, <u>Carry It On--A History in Song and Picture of the Working Men And Women of America</u>, Simon & Schuster, 1985.

Phillip Foner, <u>American Labor Songs of the Nineteenth Century</u>, University of Illinois Press, 1974.

In addition, you might compile labor struggle songs from folksingers like Holly Near, Joan Baez, Arlo Guthrie, Kate Wolf, and Claudia Schmidt. A community sing-along can raise consciousness about labor issues and create a feeling of solidarity and empowerment among participants.

3) An obvious option is to organize a demonstration to protest any current labor struggle. You may want to draft, beforehand, a legislative package, that would help initiate the labor reform you are seeking.

During the demonstration, hand out leaflets of your proposed legislative reform and urge people to encourage their legislators to initiate the reform.

4) Rent an auditorium and schedule several speakers who are active in the labor movement. You might include an opportunity for small group discussions afterwards to focus on what participants can do, on a local level, to work on the particular worker struggle.

5) An idea that I think holds a lot of promise is to hold fund-raising events, and donate the money raised to organizations fighting for workers' rights. I think this would be particularly easy to implement because it would fit right in with the ways people are already used to celebrating Labor Day. For example, you could hold barbecues, square dances, picnics, auctions, concerts, small fairs, i.e. traditional Labor Day activities, and use these recreational activities as a means to generate money for labor causes!

6) Another way I hope to observe Labor Day/May Day in the future is to schedule a conference on worker collectives. A worker collective is a business that is collectively owned and operated by its workers. Worker collectives address the issues of worker struggles in a unique way; they create industries and businesses where the workers are the owners! Thus, in a worker collective, the age old conflict--where the interests of the workers are always in conflict with the interests of the owners--is alleviated.

In such a conference I would hope to have some members of worker collectives come and speak. I have held educational seminars on worker collectives in the past and found that members of worker collectives will enthusiastically accept invitations to come and speak about the functioning of their collectives. They are also willing to assist interested people in setting up their own worker collectives.

Holding a conference about worker collectives during the week of Labor Day (or May Day), so as to encourage the formation of worker collectives in your community, is a unique way to further the struggle for workers' rights. In the final sense, until workers own the businesses that they labor in, they will always be, to some degree, exploited.

If the idea of a activist-oriented Labor Day observance sounds appealing to you, I'm sure you can add to the ideas I have listed.

The last issue I felt a need to address was whether to celebrate Labor Day on the first Monday in September or on May 1st as the rest of the world does. After reviewing the history of the two holidays, I personally decided I wanted to change my Labor Day celebration to May 1st. I think it is important for the United States to get in sync with the rest of the world. Though it is true that the first Labor Day preceded May Day by several years, had it not been for the anti-communist, anti-socialist sentiments of influential labor leaders, I think we would today be celebrating our Labor Day on May 1st. It seems easiest at this point for us to change our date than for the rest of the world to change theirs. This seems particularly so because May 1st was originally a day organized in America, by Americans, and was only later disowned because of political disagreements!

Autumn Equinox

As I have discussed previously, I observe the seasonal changes of the earth as holidays. I celebrate by getting together with friends for a pot-luck dinner, reciting poems and inspirational readings, singing, dancing and playing games. I have included a poem below, which I read at one of our Autumn Equinox celebrations, in which I try to capture the essence of the holiday:

Poem for an Autumn Equinox Pot-Luck Dinner with Friends

Today we come together to behold and partake of the earth's wisdom.
In the earth's beautiful balance and harmony we recognize, is manifest the wisdom of God.

Today is the first day of autumn.
We behold the magnificent and breath-taking colors of the trees.
As we witness with awe this transformation, we are reminded of the cycles through which we all must pass.
We are reminded that only through death comes re-birth.
We watch the individual leaves and plants die, That the future trees and forests and fields, May be born again next year.
We are thus called to understand that when someday we as individuals die, It is so our spirits can be re-born into new form, For further growth and enlightenment.

In beholding the earth's transition into autumn, The earth teaches us not only of the need for death, But also of the ongoing necessity in life of letting go of parts, That the whole may maintain its health. As we watch the trees and forests let go of the parts of themselves that have fulfilled their unique purpose, May we become more in touch with what we need to let go of in ourselves, In order to grow and blossom in new ways. May we reaffirm our understanding that culmination and moving on Are necessary for future growth and re-birth.

May we remember all that the earth teaches us today in the coming months.
May we remember to view all pain

as a catalyst for growth.
May we remain in touch with the knowledge
That each of us has a unique purpose
In the ever-changing, ever-evolving
Universe.

Let us feast and dance together to rejoice in the
divine balance and harmony of our planet
And the Universe.

You may want to consider celebrating the seasonal changes of the earth as holidays. I have found it a positive experience.

OCTOBER

Columbus Day:

Like most children in the United States, I learned about Columbus as a great hero. I memorized the names of his ships in school and learned poems like this one:

"In fourteen-hundred and ninety two
Columbus sailed the ocean blue."

However, in later years, as my reading branched beyond sugar-coated school history books, my opinion of "heros" like Columbus changed drastically. After reading books like Howard Zinn's <u>A Peoples' History of the United States</u>, I grew to look at Columbus as far less than a hero. I was further prompted to reexamine my view of Columbus when a black friend of mine remarked to me, "How in the hell can you discover a country that's already inhabited? What Columbus discovered was how to fuck over Native Americans to make a lot of money." As I became aware of the atrocities perpetrated by Columbus upon Native Americans, I was appalled at the thought of my children being taught to celebrate his birthday. I don't mean to make Columbus out to be more of an evil villain than thousands of other people; however, we don't celebrate their birthdays!

Alternative Holiday:

I presume that the reason Columbus's birthday was celebrated was that he stood for freedom from colonization and nonrepresentative government. I believe this need is covered in World Equality Day. (See listing under July.)

Halloween

Halloween is a holiday about which I knew very little. I therefore found researching its origins very interesting. After researching Halloween I decided to redesign the meaning of the holiday somewhat because I found many of the ancient Pagan and Witchcraft myths associated with Halloween, as well as the Christian adaptations of the holiday, incompatible with my values. I hope you will find my suggestions helpful.

Halloween can be traced to Druidic origins. According to the Celtic calendar, November 1st was the beginning of the new year. Thus, Halloween was originally a new year's celebration. Many aspects of the custom therefore relate to transition into the new year. The name of the holiday was originally Samhain, meaning summer's end. Many of the ceremonies pertaining to Samhain had to do with preparations for the approaching winter. The grain was gathered, animals were returned to their stalls, the sun god was thanked for the harvest, and since food supplies were abundant, a giant feast was held. It was also common to end the old year and prepare for the new by extinguishing all the hearth fires and starting new ones. The village religious leader would start a new sacred fire, and all the villagers would re-light their home hearth fires from the sacred fire.

It was also a common belief in ancient religions that the spirits of the dead came to visit the living during the changing of the year:

> *The pagan idea used to be that the crucial joints between the seasons opened cracks in the fabric of space/time allowing contact between the ghost world and the mortal one.*
>
> Barbara Walker, *The Women's Encyclopedia of Myths and Secrets*, Harper & Row, 1983, p. 372.

Thus, Samhain abounded with ideas of spirits, ghosts, and the like. Sometimes these visiting spirits were viewed as friendly. Many believed that deceased relatives came to visit on this one night of the year. It was a common custom to leave apples and nuts out for the returning spirits. Fires were lit to lead the spirits back to their ancestral homes. However, some viewed the visiting spirits of the deceased as unfriendly and vengeful. Perhaps how one viewed the visiting spirits had much to do with what kind of terms one was on with one's deceased relatives! It is believed that the custom of Halloween pranks was related to the belief in visiting spirits--one's pranks could be blamed on the visiting spirits.

The Celts also believed that Samhain was the time when the Lord of the Dead returned to Earth. Thus to appease him, sacrifices were offered: animals, usually horses, were burned. However, human criminals were also sometimes burned in wicker cages as an offering to the Lord of the Dead. Animals were also burned on Samhain because it was believed that human souls were relegated by the Lord of the Dead to live in animals' bodies for twelve months to expiate their sins. Having done their penance over the preceding year, their souls could now be released to heaven by burning the body of the animal in which they dwelled.

Samhain was also one of the eight major holidays of the religion of Witchcraft--thus the connection of witches with Halloween. The eight holidays of Witchcraft are called Sabbats and have to do with the cyclical relation of the female goddess to the male horned god. According to the myths of Witchcraft, on the Autumn equinox the male god dies, his death symbolizing the death necessary in all of nature in order for there to be continual rejuvenation and rebirth. Samhain is celebrated as the time of year when the male god visits the land of the dead, where he grows young again and is reborn through the Goddess into a new body on the Winter Solstice. The following is a Witchcraft chant for Samhain:

> *. . .To the living is revealed the Mystery: that every ending is but a new beginning. We meet in time out of time, everywhere and nowhere, here and there, to greet the Lord of Death, who is Lord of Life, and the Triple Goddess who is the circle of re-birth.*

Starhawk, *The Spiral Dance; A Rebirth of the Ancient Religion of the Great Goddess*, New York, Harper & Row, p. 181.

As Christianity took root, attempts were made by the Church to extinguish all non-Christian holiday celebrations. One of the strategies used to eradicate pagan holidays, (besides death and punishment) was to make the dates of Christian holidays, coincide with the formerly popular pagan celebrations. Thus in the eighth century, in an attempt to eliminate the celebration of Samhain, Pope Gregory III moved the Christian holiday of All Saints Day from the spring to November 1st. Through the centuries, All Hallows Eve slowly replaced the former Samhain.

Many of the current Halloween customs are a result of the Christianization of the holiday Samhain. The practice of "trick or treating" is believed to have originated from peasants going door to door in the villages asking for donations for the community feast held in honor of All Saints Day. The custom of dressing up in costumes is believed to stem from members of poor parishes dressing up to imitate saints for All Saints Day because they couldn't afford to display relics of saints as was the custom in more affluent parishes.

Doing this research about Halloween was extremely interesting to me. I had no knowledge of Halloween's pre-Christian origins or of its Christian significance. I don't recall ever being taught anything about Halloween; it was simply a time to dress up and go trick-or-treating, to soap windows, and to throw toilet paper in the yards of nasty neighbors. As an adult, I continued to enthusiastically celebrate Halloween. Instead of trick-or-treating I went to all-night costume dances and parties. However, I still attached no religious or political significance to the holiday.

Writing this book has prompted me to stop celebrating holidays mindlessly, without asking myself what I am celebrating and why. I thus felt strongly that I needed to either stop celebrating Halloween or to clarify and define what my celebration of Halloween symbolized.

I found that I did not identify with many of the Celtic, Witchcraft, or Christian interpretations of Halloween that I had learned about in my research. However, I was attracted to the idea of celebrating Halloween as a harvest festival. I therefore decided to redesign Halloween in my own mind as simply a harvest festival. I decided to keep many of the traditional ways of celebrating Halloween as part of my new holiday, because I have always enjoyed Halloween. It is so refreshing to see adults being playful! I love being greeted by bank-tellers, salespeople, waitresses etc., all dressed up in costumes. I therefore included dressing in costumes in my alternative-to-Halloween holiday and tried to capture the same air of gaiety that Halloween traditionally has had.

Alternative Holiday: Thanksgiving Harvest Festival

Since Halloween falls in October, at the close of harvest season, it was obviously well suited to being a harvest festival, and in fact, the original "Halloween" (Samhain) was partially a harvest festival. Redesigning Halloween as a harvest holiday also fit in ideally with my plans to move the holiday of Thanksgiving to an earlier time. It has always seemed to me that the celebration of Thanksgiving, at the end of November, was too far removed from actual harvest time. I realized this had to do with the mechanization of farming. In seventeenth century colonial America, it took until the end of November to harvest the crops. Thus, when Thanksgiving was declared a holiday, it came at the end of several months of strenuous, nonstop, harvesting activities. All the food was processed and stored, and there was finally time to celebrate and rejoice that enough food had

143

been harvested to last through the coming winter.

With today's farming methods, by the end of November, people have long forgotten about the fall's harvest, and it is difficult to rekindle feelings of thankfulness about the harvest. With all this in mind, I decided to move my celebration of Thanksgiving to fall on Halloween. Thus, I would redefine Halloween to be a Harvest Thanksgiving festival.

My observance of Thanksgiving Harvest Festival will thus include the traditional way of celebrating Thanksgiving--a large dinner with foods of the harvest and prayers of appreciation for the bountiful harvest--and incorporate traditional Halloween activities such as dressing in costumes and dancing all night. The costume donning and dancing can simply serve as an additional means of expressing thankfulness and joy about the harvest.

I was again chided by my family and friends for being presumptuous enough to think I have the right to meddle with three hundred-year-old holidays! However, I strongly feel that holidays need to be updated to reflect the realities of people's lives. I therefore went ahead with my plans to move my Thanksgiving celebration to fall on Halloween. Much to my surprise and satisfaction, I discovered that Canada had beat me to the idea of moving Thanksgiving to an earlier time. I found the following statement in a book about holidays in the United States and Canada:

> For a while, Canada and the United States observed Thanksgiving on the same Thursday in November. . . .In 1931, however, it was felt that November is too late in the year for an authentic harvest celebration, so the date [of Thanksgiving in Canada] was moved to the second Monday in October, which is now the accepted date.
>
> Robert Meyer Jr., *Festivals of the U.S.A. and Canada*, New York, Ives Washburn Inc., 1967, p. 153.

So, who knows, maybe my idea of moving Thanksgiving to the date of Halloween, and combining the two holidays will become so popular that the U.S. government will officially change the date of Thanksgiving! In the meantime I feel good about celebrating these holidays in ways that are meaningful to me.

NOVEMBER

Thanksgiving:

See discussion of Thanksgiving under Halloween above.

DECEMBER

Winter Solstice

As I mentioned earlier, I have been celebrating the cycles of the earth for several years now. I come together with friends for a pot-luck dinner. We read poems and sing songs and engage in recreational activities like square dancing and community games. I have included below a poem I wrote which I recited at one of the Winter Solstice dinners I participated in. I believe it captures the essence of the holiday.

Winter Solstice Poem

Today we come together to behold and partake of the earth's wisdom.

In the earth's beautiful balance and harmony, we recognize, is manifest the wisdom of God.

Today is the first day of winter. We witness the earth begin the process of turning its energies inward for replenishment and rejuvenation. We are reminded that the blooming and reawakening of spring and summer and the bounty of autumn's harvest are sustained only through the rejuvenation of winter.

We are inspired to refocus and redirect our energies inwardly to refresh ourselves, that our spirits may also be strengthened and rekindled.

As the earth holds within it through winter the seeds that shall bloom in spring, so we hold within us today, the seeds for the dreams and goals we shall give life to in the future.

As the earth cares for and nurtures its seeds, let us also nurture the potential that lies within ourselves for continual rebirth of our greater selves.

As we appreciate the cycles of the earth, let us learn to trust in our own rhythms and cycles. As we acknowledge and respect that the earth must sometimes be in cold and darkness, but will always return again to warmth and light, let us renew our faith that each of us will always come out of times of personal darkness, back into illumination.

As we again attune ourselves to the wondrous harmony of nature, our faith in a Divine purpose is ever renewed. We are reassured that pain is but a step in growth, death a catalyst for rebirth, and rebirth eternal.

We are reawakened to a knowledge and faith that each and every one of us has a unique and invaluable place in God's universe.

As the earth has begun its winter rejuvenation process, so shall we today begin the rejuvenation of our spirits through feasting and dancing together.

You may want to consider celebrating the seasons of the earth. You might find additional ideas for seasonal celebrations in books about Witchcraft or Native American rituals.

Christmas

A major cause of my increasing dissatisfaction with traditional holidays was my growing away from Christianity (see chapter 1). Since Christianity is the entire basis of Christmas, after deciding I was not a Christian, I of course had many misgivings about continuing to participate in the celebration of Christmas. Yet for many years after I knew I was not a Christian, I did, in fact, continue to celebrate Christmas. Year after year, I somehow got caught up in the hustle and bustle of Christmas. Amid the frenzy of Christmas shopping, putting up a tree, wrapping presents, having company, and baking and cooking, I simply didn't take time to address the meaning of Christmas. I knew many other people like myself who didn't consider themselves Christians, who continued nonetheless to celebrate Christmas.

Deciding to write this book was of course a decision to confront my confusion, dissatisfaction, and ambivalence about all the rituals that I was participating in, including holidays. So there loomed Christmas, to be at last confronted and grappled with. Whether I liked it or not, I was going to sort out my thoughts and feelings about Christmas.

I began by realizing that part of the reason I clung to the idea of celebrating Christmas was that, though I wasn't a Christian, I believed that Jesus had been an extremely spiritually enlightened being, and I found many of his teachings very inspiring. I had always used Christmas as a time to try to live the teachings of Jesus [that I agreed with] more fully. I tried to become more loving, more giving to the needy, less judgmental, and less violent. Yet I had a growing sense of dissatisfaction about celebrating Christmas.

My dissatisfaction, I began to clarify, stemmed from the fact that though I agreed with some of the teachings of Jesus, I had come to disagree with many others, and with many teachings in The Bible in general. Christianity promoted ideas I considered unhealthy, like sexism, rigidity, hierarchy, and a view of humanity as evil. I came to have far more disagreements with Christianity than compatibilities. I therefore became uncomfortable with participating in Christian rituals. I recognized that by continuing to participate in them, I was furthering Christianity's influence in our society, which made little sense, considering my sentiments.

With regard to Christmas in particular, I realized that my beliefs were completely at odds with the religious meaning of the holiday. The religious basis for Christmas is to celebrate Jesus as the Christ, the divine messenger from God The Father, and this is why most people continue to celebrate it today. I do not share this belief. To begin with, as I outlined in chapter 1, I do not view God as a male; I find the idea of "God the Father in Heaven" an archaic and extremely sexist concept. Secondly, I do not believe God sends messengers in the sense portrayed in Christianity, and therefore I do not believe Jesus to have been a messenger from God.

I realized that by celebrating Christmas, I was reinforcing the idea of Jesus as "the Christ," which I did not believe. By celebrating Jesus's birthday as a holiday, I was reinforcing the idea of him being a special teacher. Though I did view Jesus as a great teacher, there were many other spiritual teachers that I revered as highly as Jesus, yet I did not celebrate their birthdays as holidays. As I contemplated how long the list of my spiritual teachers was, the absurdity of celebrating all their birthdays became quickly obvious.

What I slowly began to realize was that I needed a holiday that did not have as its focus a particular person or persons. What would make much more sense to me was a holiday that had as its focus the spiritual teachings of people like Jesus. What I believed to be the basic focus of Jesus's teachings, as well as many other spiritual teachers, was how to attune oneself with God. Thus, I wanted to design an alternative holiday to Christmas that had this broader idea--of attuning oneself to God rather than the birth of Jesus as its basis.

I decided to design my holiday to be a week long one because I planned to have it encompass the New Year's holiday as well. All the ideas I was formulating about my alternative holiday fit very well with the idea of beginning the new year. In addition, I felt that in our society we do not take enough time off from the hustle and bustle of our lives for meditation, spiritual attunement, or just plain fun. Thus, I thought it would be a good idea to take a week off at the end of the year for these purposes.

I pondered for some time what to call my alternative holiday. I eventually settled upon the name "Week of Attunement" because I thought that captured the essence of what I envisioned the holiday to be. The word "attune," I discovered, was of Latin origin, meaning to move toward harmony. I defined the purpose of Week of Attunement as follows:

A time to prepare oneself for the challenges of the coming year, by bringing oneself into greater attunement with God. *

Some people might feel more comfortable phrasing this concept as tuning into the loving source of the universe, the Goddess, The Great Spirit, the Higher Self, or the God within. I believe that all human beings are manifestations of God; I therefore envisioned the holiday to be a time to become more in tune with love for family and friends, and humanity in general. Since I believe that a part of God resides in every individual, I also wanted to design the Week of Attunement to be a time to tune into the inner self; to explore one's deepest feelings and thoughts.

I next began to tackle the logistics of my new holiday. I had to decide what activities and methods I was going to propose for achieving the purpose I had defined. As I brainstormed about what activities to include in my Week of Attunement holiday, I decided to examine the traditional activities of Christmas and New Year's celebrations to determine if I wanted to adapt any of these customs.

I first considered whether I wanted to include gift-giving during Week of Attunement. Through the years I had become more and more disillusioned with gift-giving at Christmas. I became so disgusted with the constant barrage of glossy newspaper advertisements, radio and television advertisements, and store displays urging me to buy, buy, buy, that I found it difficult to feel any joy in buying presents. In addition, I often found it extremely difficult to think of anything that family members or friends would want or need. As a result, it became a chore to pick out gifts. Likewise, I often received gifts that I really didn't like and they ended up collecting dust in a closet. Last, I found it difficult to recover from the hundreds of dollars I usually spent on Christmas. Really, I always felt that I couldn't afford to participate in Christmas! So I seriously considered discontinuing gift exchanging when I gave up Christmas, and was skeptical about including gift-giving in my new holiday. However, after having a discussion with a friend about the custom of gift-giving, I began to view it differently.

I realized that the custom of gift-giving actually had a noble and positive purpose. I began to realize that gift-giving is meant to be an expression of love and caring. It is a way of saying that I appreciate you as a person, and that I'm glad you are my friend, a part of my family, etc. The problem is that the custom

---

*God is a word that means many different things to many different people. Please see chapter 1 for my definition of the word.

of gift-giving is so distorted and contaminated by our excessive cultural materialism that it becomes difficult to even remember that gift-giving is meant to be an act of love.

I concluded that gift-giving could be a very positive part of a holiday celebration, if it was not practiced as it typically is in our society. I realized that the idea of gift-giving actually fit in very well with the concept of my Week of Attunement holiday. Attuning oneself with one's love for family and friends was one of the holiday's purposes so giving gifts as an expression of that love made a lot of sense.

I therefore decided to include the exchange of gifts as part of my holiday celebration. However, I made an agreement with myself that I would henceforth give gifts according to the following guidelines:

1) When buying gifts I will spend within a realistic budget based on my income, not on some American fantasy of the perfect Christmas gift.

2) I will talk openly with family and friends and set a price range for how much we will spend on gifts to one another that we both feel comfortable with.

3) I will give practical gifts instead of buying useless trinkets because I can't think of what to buy a person. For example, I have started giving gift baskets of little things like cheese, maple syrup, jellies, candies, teas, soaps, socks, pens, stationery, pot-holders, kitchen towels, etc. I find I can make these baskets for a fraction of the cost of buying pre-made ones. Last year I carried my philosophy of practical gifts a step further: I gave my sister five nice wooden clothes hangers. She laughed hysterically when she opened them, but thought they were great! Many people appreciate practical gifts. Gift certificates are also nice gifts. I particularly like to give certificates from book stores.

4) When I don't know what someone needs I will call and ask their spouse or roommate for ideas instead of guessing.

5) I will talk with family members and friends honestly about what gifts they like and don't like, so we can get better through the years at buying for one another. I will encourage returning unwanted gifts. For the last five years I have made this easy by leaving all tags on gifts and packing the receipt in the box. I see no problem letting people know what things cost. I think that it is an impractical custom to remove tags from gifts.

6) I will allow myself ample time to do my shopping. I have found that if I procrastinate in my shopping so that I have to do it at the last minute I start buying things just to get it done. I have found that if I go to malls when they are not crowded, or shop in small, "alternative" stores, I do a much better job of shopping.

7) I WILL NOT MAKE GIFT EXCHANGING THE PRIMARY FOCUS OF THE HOLIDAY!!!!!

8) The last change I made regarding gift-giving is that I bought some brightly colored cotton calico, and sewed a bunch of gift bags of all

sizes that are completely reusable. After I give gifts, I take back the bag. I estimate I will be able to use the same bags for at least ten years! I found this a good solution to the dilemma of throw-away expensive wrapping paper which seems like such a waste of resources. I went through a period of giving gifts wrapped in brown paper bags and newspapers, and though it may have been ecological, it did take a good deal of aesthetic pleasure out of gift-giving! The many colored cotton calico gift bags look very beautiful piled in our living room.

The next traditional Christmas activity that I examined was decorating a Christmas tree. This was an aspect of Christmas I knew I was going to miss. I had many wonderful family memories of picking out a tree and joyfully hanging all the ornaments that had been passed down from my grandparents, or that my parents had collected through the years. In addition, my partner was a little skeptical when I suggested to him that I no longer wanted to have a Christmas tree. Although my partner very much supports my writing this book and does not consider himself a Christian, he lamented that our children would not have the joyful experience of decorating a tree, because he himself had so many beautiful childhood memories about it. I assured him that we could design some way of celebrating Week of Attunement that would be as thrilling as going out into the woods as a family and chopping down a pine tree and decorating it.

I was well aware that many people continued to have Christmas trees though they no longer considered themselves Christians. Several people have, in fact, informed me that decorating trees was actually a pagan custom which was later Christianized. However, to me and 99 percent of the other people in this culture, a decorated pine tree is a "Christmas tree." I personally felt it would be impossible to redefine a decorated pine tree to not be a symbol of Christianity. I therefore decided I wanted to design something completely new as an alternative to a Christmas tree.

Though my partner was a little skeptical he agreed to help me, being the wonderfully open-minded person that he is. After quite a bit of brainstorming wonderful ideas began to take shape in my head. One of the main functions of a Christmas tree was to provide a place to put gifts. Since I intended for my holiday to include the exchange of gifts, I wanted my Christmas tree alternative to include a place to put gifts. Another benefit that having a Christmas tree offered was the opportunity for a family to go out in the woods together. I hoped to be able to incorporate this into whatever alternative I designed.

What evolved out of my brainstorming was the idea of an "attunement wheel," a seven foot wooden wheel that sits in one's living room. In front of the wheel we made a giant basket woven out of pine branches, into which we put gifts. We decorated the wheel with dried flowers, corn husks, and pine branches. We also hung a few ornaments and blinking lights. There is also a small shelf on the wheel with a candle for each member of the family. Instead of stockings, we each hung a basket on the wheel. In the baskets we put the nonmaterial gifts we are giving to each other in the coming year--things like love letters, notes of appreciation, and pledges to one another for the coming year.

I think our attunement wheel has all the wonderful aspects of a Christmas tree without its negative ones. Instead of having to chop down a tree, we just cut a few branches off of several large pine trees. This way the tree does not die; we just harvest a few branches from it each year. We still get to go out into the woods as a family, and no doubt the children we intend to have will have many beautiful memories about decorating attunement wheels through the years. Most importantly my attunement wheel is not a symbol of Christianity. The wheel is a great stimulus for discussion too. When people come over, they ask about it, and I

An

Attunement

Wheel

We take this time to
attune ourselves to the
truths of the Universe.
Let us look inward to discover
the deepest callings of our Souls.

Let us commune with one another
sharing our spiritual revelations so as to
help one another more fully manifest
our potential as human beings.

May the giving of these
gifts be a reflection of the

Love and understanding we
strive to give one
another each day of
Our lives.

have the opportunity to share with them the changes I have undergone regarding rituals.

The next part of the holiday I needed to think about was the family dinner. I knew I wanted to include a family dinner/gathering as part of my Week of Attunement. However there were some significant changes I wanted to make about the manner in which I had celebrated Christmas through the years.

Since I have been a vegetarian for ten years, I no longer feel comfortable serving ham or turkey for holiday dinners. I therefore discussed with my family how they would feel about eating something vegetarian for Christmas dinner. I happily discovered that my family was open to the idea of vegetarian dinners for the holidays. They agreed that as long as I did the cooking, they were willing to eat vegetarian food on holidays for my sake. I am now having lots of fun trying to think up fancy, festive dinners like stuffed artichokes!

However, on the other side of my family, is my partner's father, whom I have been unable to convert to vegetarianism even for one day a year. He is willing, however, to make special baked beans for me without pork. I also have great fun imitating his meat dishes with vegetarian counterparts. For the last thirty years, he has made "pigs in a blanket" with pork sausage on Christmas Eve. I counter that with "piggies" made out of tempeh with pickled ginger! I have also concocted a Fabulous Figgie Pudding that is completely dairyless, using tofu.

The next Christmas custom that I found I had to adapt in order to suit my new holiday was singing Christmas carols. I realized it made no sense for me to continue singing songs about a Christ that I didn't even believe existed! Yet I knew I would really miss this family singing: my family had sung Christmas carols together since I was old enough to sing. I therefore decided to put together a list of songs that my partner and I could begin designating as Week of Attunement songs and that we could eventually teach our children. I hope to add to the following list:

> "Imagine"--John Lennon
> "What the World Needs Now Is Love"--Hal David
> "Song of The Soul"--Cris Williamson
> "Thanksgiving Eve"--Sally Rogers
> "If I Had a Hammer"--Lee Hays and Pete Seeger
> "All You Need Is Love"--The Beatles
> "Teach Your Children" Crosby, Stills, Nash, and Young
> "Put A Little Love In Your Heart"--Jackie De Shannon

After adapting various customs from Christmas, I then contemplated what new activities I wanted to include in my Week of Attunement holiday. I decided I wanted to add a serious aspect to the holiday. The gift-giving, singing, and dinner were all important but I also wanted to deal with the spiritual aspect of the holiday.

I therefore added to my family celebration of Week of Attunement the practice of sitting together in a circle and reciting poems or inspirational readings, having to do with the concept of attunement. I have included three sample readings that I have used. There are of course an infinite number of poems/readings that one could use.

Untitled Poem

I am called upon to, and am committed to,
*   bring myself and ourselves continually more into harmony*
with Universe.
*   I am doing this by--*
experimenting with ways of perceiving and interacting--
*   with each other, with all be-ings, Gaia and Universe,*
Which, by the very nature of those ways,
create flow in the direction of--weave into be-ing--coming to balance.
*   Some of the ways I am now exploring include:*
*   Learning/teaching who We are,*
*   Naming, calling forth our best selves;*
Nurturing the child within, the wonderment, the playfulness;
*   Loving Universe/Ourselves, accepting what-is, trusting;*
Receiving, healing the hurts and imbalances, forgiving, sharing,
*   feeling, intuiting;*
*   Celebrating, singing the be-ing, the life cycles, the*
weaving of what-is;
*   Participating in life, giving, negotiating, challenging,*
risking, making mistakes, becoming humble, dis-covering,
empowering;
*   Honoring/"grokking" the gifts other beings offer us in*
becoming our "food"
*   and the gifts we offer in each moment-by-moment participation;*
*   Listening for, and respecting all perspectives, trying on*
the others' shoes, acknowledging
*   and un-learning the assumptions*
*   Acknowledging arrogance, creating space;*
Creating visions of the balance--
*   alternative energy sources,*
appropriate technologies, local material-goods production,
*   organic gardens, co-ops, re-cycling materials,*
*   community, consensus decision-making,*
*   "right livelihood",*
new (old?) languages of the spirit,
*   new (old) economies that support heart values,*
Re-discovering and Re-creating Our Place In The Universe.

Christopher Coon, Unpublished Poem, Ann Arbor Michigan, 1984.
Reprinted with permission.

151

Desiderata

Go placidly amid the noise and the haste,
And remember what peace there may be in silence.
As far as possible without surrender be on good
terms with all persons.
Speak your truth quietly and clearly; And listen to others,
even to the dull and the ignorant;
They too have their story.
Avoid loud and aggressive persons, they are vexatious
to the spirit.
If you compare yourself with others,
you may become vain or bitter;
for always there will be greater and lesser persons than yourself.
Enjoy your achievements as well as your plans.
Keep interested in your own career, however humble;
it is a real possession in the changing fortunes of time.
Exercise caution in your business affairs; for the
world is full of trickery.
But let this not blind you to what virtue there is;
many persons strive for high ideals; and everywhere
life is full of heroism.
Be yourself. Especially, do not feign affection.
Neither be cynical about love; for in the face of all aridity
and disenchantment it is as perennial as the grass.
Take kindly the counsel of the years, gracefully surrendering
the things of youth.
Nurture strength of spirit to shield you in sudden
misfortune.
But do not distress yourself with dark imaginings.
Many fears are born of fatigue and loneliness.
Beyond a wholesome discipline, be gentle with yourself.
You are a child of the universe, no less than the trees
and the stars;
You have a right to be here.
And whether or not it is clear to you,
no doubt the universe is unfolding as it should.
Therefore be at peace with God, whatever you conceive Him
[Her] to be.
And whatever your labors and aspirations,
in the noisy confusion of life keep peace in your soul.
With all its sham, drudgery and broken dreams,
it is still a beautiful world.
Be cheerful. Strive to be happy.

EVER RETHINKING THE LORD'S PRAYER

June 12, 1979

Our God--
Since omni-experience is your identity
You have given us
overwhelming manifest:--
of Your complete knowledge
of Your complete comprehension
of Your complete concern
of Your complete coordination
of Your complete responsibility
of Your complete capability to cope
in absolute wisdom and effectiveness
with all problems and events
and of Your eternally unfailing reliability
so to do.

Yours, Dear God,
is the only and complete glory.

By Glory I mean
the synergetic totality
of all physical and metaphysical radiation
and of all physical and metaphysical gravity
of finite
but nonunitarily conceptual
scenario Universe
in whose synergetic totality
the a priori energy potentials
of both radiation and gravity
are initially equal
but whose respective
behavioral patterns are such
than radiation's entropic, redundant disintegratings
is always less effective
that gravity's nonredundant
syntropic integrating

Radiation is plural and differentiable,
radiation is focusable, beamable, and self-sinusing,
is interceptible, separatist, and biasable--
ergo, has shadowed voids and vulnerabilities;

Gravity is unit and undifferentiable
Gravity is comprehensive
inclusively embracing and permeative
is non-focusable and shadowless,
and is omni-integrative;
all of which characteristics of gravity
are also the characteristics of love.
Love is metaphysical gravity.
You, dear God,
are the totally loving intellect

ever designing
and ever daring to test
and thereby irrefutably proving
to the uncompromising satisfaction
of Your own comprehensive and incisive
knowledge of the absolute truth
that Your generalized principles
adequately accommodate any and all
special case developments,
involvements, and side effects;
wherefore Your absolutely courageous
omnirigorous and ruthless self-testing
alone can and does absolutely guarantee
total conservation
of the integrity
of eternally regenerative Universe

Your eternally regenerative scenario Universe
is the minimum complex
of totally intercomplementary
totally intertransforming
nonsimultaneous, differently frequenced
and differently enduring
feedback closures
of a finite
but nonunitarily
nonsimultaneously conceptual system
in which naught is created
and naught is lost
and all occurs
in optimum efficiency.

Total accountability and total feedback
constitute the minimum and only
perpetual motion system.
Universe is the one and only
eternally regenerative system.

To accomplish Your regenerative integrity
You give Yourself the responsibility
of eternal, absolutely continuous,
tirelessly vigilant wisdom.

Wherefore we have absolute faith and trust in You,
and we worship You
awe-inspiredly,
all-thankfully,
rejoicingly,
lovingly,
Amen.

R. Buckminster Fuller, Critical Path, New York, St.
Martin's Press Inc., 1981, pp. 153-158, Copyright 1981
by R. Buckminster Fuller. Reprinted with permission.

I may decide in the future to expand the idea of coming together to read poems about "attunement" into a community worship service, instead of a private one with just my family.

That pretty much took care of replacing Christmas as a holiday. However, I had designed Week of Attunement to be a week-long holiday, which included New Year's Eve and Day. I thus needed to think about how I wanted to redesign my New Year's celebration.

Though I was always one to enjoy the gaiety and dancing of a good New Years Eve party (minus the alcohol), I had always felt that there should be a serious side to the holiday. Therefore, I decided that in addition to celebrating New Year's with dancing and general merriment I would design some serious activities to add to my Week of Attunement observance--activities that would address the spiritual aspect of the holiday: attuning oneself for the new year. I came up with the following methods: individual meditation and group attunement.

Individual Meditation

Meditation is, of course, a very ancient practice. There are many, many forms of meditation, ranging from thinking quietly to oneself about whatever comes to mind, to more disciplined, regimented forms using mantras or other specific methods. I have in general found the more free-form meditation more suited to my personality, though I sometimes do include some form of structure in my meditation. For the Week of Attunement meditation I felt that I did want to use some structured exercises as opposed to totally free-flow meditation. I therefore decided upon the following Values Clarification questions for my Week of Attunement meditation:

1) What do I understand the purpose of my life to be?

2) When during the last year have I felt the most in harmony and connection with God/the universe? The most out of harmony?

3) What changes can I make in the ways I am living to bring myself more in tune with God?

My meditation consists of lying quietly for several hours meditating upon these questions. I try to open myself to communication with God or my higher self. I also usually read some poetry or a book by someone I believe to be very much in harmony with God using the information as inspiration and guidance. Finally, since I feel closest to God when I am in the woods, I always include a long walk in the woods alone as part of my individual meditation.

I then move on to more specific questions:

1) The three most fun experiences I had this past year were. . .

2) The three most painful experiences I had this past year were. . . What I learned from them were. . .

3) The five accomplishments I feel happy about achieving this year are. . .

4) Some positive changes I've made in my relationships with people this year are. . .

5) Five important things I've learned about myself this past year are. . .

6) Three positive changes in my lifestyle that I've made this year are. . .

7) Five gifts or contributions that I've made to other people/the world this past year are. . .

8) Some things that come to mind that I wanted to do this past year that I didn't have time for are...

9) If I magically had unlimited time, energy, and money to do every single thing I wanted to do this coming year, I would do the following fifty things (include both fun, and work/accomplishment type things).

10) If I had only this coming year to live, how would I spend it?

I find the hours I put into doing these exercises well worth the time. They help me to get in touch with where I'm at with myself and my life. I use all the answers to these Values Clarification exercises to formulate my goals for the new year. However, I form my new year's goals in my "Group Attunement Meeting" discussed next.

Group Attunement Meeting

A group attunement meeting is perhaps the most exciting part of my new holiday. I designed the attunement group meeting to be very similar to a personal growth seminar. In creating its structure and format, I was inspired by two therapists I know in Ann Arbor, Bob and Margaret Blood. For over ten years, Bob and Margaret have at the end of each December held a "New Year's Retreat." The description in their brochure for the workshop is very similar to how I would describe my Week of Attunement group meeting:

This workshop is for those who wish to take time out to use the turn of the year as an occasion for personal reflection and meaningful sharing. We will review the journeys we have traveled during the past year to see what we have learned. We will re-assess our priorities to discover whether we are spending our energies in the ways in which we feel most deeply called. We will dare to express our hopes for the year ahead and will envision the steps we can take to make those hopes come true. Throughout the weekend we will balance our serious work with joyful celebration of the gift of another year. . . .We hope to leave the workshop refreshed and inspired by our own individual work, by our insights into the lives of others, and by the atmosphere of warmth and caring.

Bob and Margaret Blood, December 1985. Reprinted with permission.

The format I use for my Week of Attunement group meeting is very similar to Bob and Margaret's workshop except that I just meet with a group of friends, with no facilitator per se. In the past I have participated in group seminars with a professional therapist facilitating, and I found those groups a fantastic learning experience. However, I tend not to use professional facilitators in the groups I now participate in. I have taken quite a few classes in group process skills, and I have had enough experiences in groups, so that I feel confident using a leaderless group format. Likewise, most of my friends have had training in group process. My friends and I rotate the facilitation role in our group attunement meeting.

If you decide to have a New Year's group meeting you may want to hire a professional leader/therapist, or you may want to use the leaderless group format. The decision as to whether or not to use a professional facilitator should be based on your own and other members' group process skills. For a discussion of the pros and cons of leaderless vs. leader facilitated groups, see chapter 2.

Though you should certainly feel free to use your own ideas and imagination if you decide to conduct an attunement group, I offer the following outline to give you some ideas of what has worked well for me.

Suggested Format for Week of Attunement Group Meeting

<u>Size:</u>
I think this type of group functions best with six to ten people.

<u>Timeframe:</u>
I like to set up at least two four-hour sessions for the meeting, e.g., a morning and an afternoon session, with a break for lunch. I have found the weekend or all-day format for group seminars more helpful than a one-night three-hour session, because there is enough time for the group to get acquainted, do some significant "work", and to wrap up the session.

<u>Preparation:</u>
I have found it is helpful to hand out written exercises to group participants before the group meeting. Last year when I was the facilitator of the New Year's group meeting, I handed out the Values Clarification exercises that I use in my individual meditation (just discussed). As I stated earlier, I find these structured exercises very helpful, and in a group setting they really help to focus the group's energies.

<u>Meeting Process:</u>
It is difficult to capture in words the process of any group meeting. It is difficult to say, first you do this, then this happens; group process is flowing and spontaneous. However, what ultimately happens in a New Year's Attunement Group is that each member in turn shares their answers to the Values Clarification questions that have been handed out beforehand. From there, group members help one another to set up goals for the new year.

Group members help one another with their goal setting in a variety of ways. First, group members provide one another with a supportive and therapeutic environment in which members can explore their innermost thoughts and feelings. Second, as group members listen to one another's dreams, goals, and hopes, they can serve as inspiration to one another.

Another important way group members help one another in setting up goals for the new year is that they confront one another when any group member attempts to set unrealistic, inappropriate goals for himself/herself. People often use New Year's as a hey-day for self-flagellation, and group members can help confront this self-destructive behavior. Group members can also confront a member who seems to be setting goals to please or appease others, rather than setting goals that he/she wants to accomplish. All of this confrontation, by the way, should be of a gentle, nurturing kind.

In general, group members help one another define the directions they want to take with their lives in the coming year, and help one another set healthy goals for moving in those directions.

That sums up the changes I have made in my life regarding holiday celebrations. Since I redesigned the holiday rituals I participate in, I have found that I look forward to holidays. This is a refreshing change; I used to be so dissatisfied with holiday celebrations that I dreaded every holiday. I also look forward to celebrating holidays with my children; I feel excited about teaching them the religious and political significance of the holiday rituals they are participating in.

I hope the information I presented will help those of you dissatisfied with traditional holidays to design new holidays that are more in tune with your needs. I hope you find the process as rewarding as I did.

Comments and suggestions about this book are welcomed
by the author. Please address to:

Susan M. Mumm
Quantum Leap Publishing & Distributing
P.O. Box 7916
Ann Arbor, Michigan 48107